Writing Lessons for the Overhead

Grade 1

by Lola M. Schaefer

New York • Toronto • London • Auckland • Sydney
Mexico City • New Delhi • Hong Kong • Buenos Aires

Teaching *Resources*

For dedicated writing teachers—
your modeling and mini-lessons help create lifelong writers

Acknowledgments

My appreciation to my editors Joanna Davis-Swing and Sarah Longhi,
who work hard to publish the best resources for teachers.

Cover design by Lillian Kohli
Interior design by Sarah Morrow

2 3 4 5 6 7 8 9 10   40   12 11 10 09 08 07 06

Contents

Introduction..4

    The Tools of Self-Expression...............................4

    How to Use the Samples in This Book.....................5

Chapter 1 ✳ Journal Entries...............................6

Chapter 2 ✳ Meaning......................................12

Chapter 3 ✳ Focus..18

Chapter 4 ✳ Organization................................25

Chapter 5 ✳ Vocabulary..................................37

Chapter 6 ✳ Details......................................45

Chapter 7 ✳ Leads..53

Chapter 8 ✳ Revision....................................64

Bibliography...79

Index...80

Introduction

The Tools of Self-Expression

First-grade writers are enthusiastic. They have much to say and are eager to learn how to express themselves. They want to share stories of family, friends, and pets—not to mention all of the important events of their lives. We need to create nurturing classroom environments that support their first efforts and offer instruction that will help them grow as writers.

While working as a consultant, I see that even the youngest student writers want tools—ways to improve their writing skills. Because my time is often limited in classrooms, I've developed short examples of grade-appropriate writing that pinpoint specific elements of craft. I use these samples in mini-lessons designed to help student writers discover the differences between poor and strong writing. While displaying a set of writing samples on an overhead projector, I question the students about one of the following: journal entries, meaning, focus, organization, vocabulary, details, leads, or revision.

Engagement is high during these mini-lessons. I read the pieces aloud two or three times so the students can first familiarize themselves with the content. Then we examine the writing more closely on successive reads. They home in on the qualities that make the strong writing sample compelling and clear. As I ask questions, they begin to recognize which leads intrigue them and offer the reader necessary information. They realize that specific word choice adds to the meaning and provides pictures to the audience. They learn that tight focus is a tool a writer uses to keep the reader involved in the text. They find the beginnings, middles, and ends in different genres and see how these logically order a piece of writing. They celebrate that well-chosen details add information and ideas to an otherwise blah piece of writing. They also note that if the reader doesn't understand the text, there are ways to clarify meaning.

I've learned over the years that it isn't just the well-written pieces that help cement this understanding. It's the contrast between poorly written pieces and well-written pieces that pushes students to be more critical thinkers. I always enjoy seeing how young writers scoff at the lack of detail or the boring vocabulary they find in weak writing and then firmly decide that they won't write like that. And they don't. The quality of their writing improves quickly. They begin to avoid the pitfalls that we have studied and discussed and to write using the strongest piece as their gold standard. The companion mini-lessons provide tools—examples and strategies to bring about such changes.

How to Use the Samples in This Book

The pieces contained in this book are designed to help you present mini-lessons to your first graders on eight key elements of craft that will help them begin their journey toward producing proficient and original writing. The mini-lesson format offers a brief (4- to 12-minute) instructional lesson to focus children at the beginning of a writing workshop or writing period.

The purpose is to share one writing strategy, procedure, example, or insight in a way that makes the ideas stick and without overwhelming the children. Some children will be ready for the information and use it almost immediately in their writing. Others will need more practice and mini-lessons before they employ your teaching point.

> Remember, all student writers come to you with their own unique backgrounds in literacy. Each mini-lesson plants a seed in their minds. It will sprout and take root when the writer has the understanding and practice to make it meaningful for him or her.

The chapters that follow provide you with a detailed teaching plan, including a model mini-lesson and samples written at a first-grade reading and interest level. You can use the writing samples and lesson ideas to

1. introduce a new craft element to your students.

2. reinforce efforts you've seen your students make.

3. nudge students into revision with one craft element in mind.

I have found the greatest results when I use one set of samples over the course of a two- to three-week period. Revisiting the same samples while children are writing their own pieces helps children recognize, practice, and apply a specific craft element before adding another. That doesn't mean you won't revisit similar lessons again in the future. You probably will. But I encourage you to immerse children in the language and practice of one element before moving on to another.

The anonymity of the pieces helps create a nonthreatening atmosphere in the classroom. Children can critically examine and evaluate the samples with no worry of insult or humiliation. These pieces are simply working models, with no personal consequences of fame or shame for any one child.

We teach the tools of writing so students will be able to express their thoughts and ideas. Use these samples to enhance your students' understanding of the craft of writing. Then step back and encourage them to write passionately about what they know and feel. For it's when students are emotionally involved in their own pieces that they are likely to reexamine their writing with a critical eye and find opportunities to use these strategies.

In this set of writing samples from Chapter 2, all three paragraphs describe the life cycle of a tadpole. The first and third samples are written in a vague, confusing way, while the second is clearly written and easier to understand. Comparing the stronger sample with the weaker ones helps children understand the lesson focus: how writers use specific details to make their writing meaningful to a reader.

CHAPTER 1

Journal Entries

THE QUESTION TO EXPLORE

Do I Hear a Who, What, and Something Interesting?

Many first graders begin the year by writing in journals. By definition, journals are records of observations and occurrences. Children need to be writing in their journals frequently, describing what they see and do. With self-selected topics, they will have an endless supply of ideas. I always ask that children include *who*, *what*, and *something interesting* in their journal entries. And this is how I often introduce those criteria.

Introducing Journal Writing: Who, What, and Something Interesting

Before this mini-lesson, draw a colorful picture of you doing something you enjoy (use the top half of a sheet of chart paper). Make sure to include a few details in your picture. For example, if you're riding a bike, show houses or trees in the background. Place the sun or clouds in the sky. If your bike has special features, add them.

Begin your mini-lesson on journal entries like this:

Teacher: Today I would like you to help me write a message in my journal. Last night I drew this picture. Please, tell me who is in my picture.

Student: Is that you?

Teacher: Yes.

Student: Is that a friend with you?

Teacher: Yes, that's my husband. Now, can you tell me what I'm doing?

Student: You are fishing.

Teacher: Yes, that's correct. So, the who of my picture is *my husband and I.*

The what of my picture is *fishing*. I want to make sure I get those two pieces of information in my message today. Now, I could write: **My husband and I like to fish.** But I would like to add something interesting to my message. Do you notice any details in my picture?

Student: You're both in a boat.

Teacher: Yes, I could write: **My husband and I often fish from a boat.** Do you notice anything else?

Student: You've got a fish on your line, but your husband doesn't.

Teacher: Yes. I could add that information. I could write: **My husband and I went fishing in a boat. I caught more fish than he did.** Is there anything else that you notice in the picture?

Student: It's a sunny day.

Teacher: Yes, it is. I could write: **One sunny day, my husband and I went fishing in a boat. I caught more fish than he did.** Is there anything else you see in the picture?

Student: I can see land and trees behind your boat. Are you on a river or on a lake?

Teacher: We like to fish on lakes. Now, I could write: **One sunny day, my husband and I went fishing in a boat out on a lake. I caught more fish than he did.** I could write that, or I could write something simpler. What I need are these three things. I need the who. Who am I going to write about?

Student: You and your husband.

Teacher: That's right. And what are we doing?

Student: You're fishing.

Teacher: I must remember to add that information. Now, I need to write something interesting. Should I write that it was a sunny day, that I caught more fish than my husband, that we fished in a boat, or that it was on a lake?

Student: Make sure you write that you caught more fish than he did.

Teacher: OK, I will do that. Now, I'm going to say what I want to write.

Take a moment and say what you want to write in a couple of different ways. Children need to see you think out loud.

Teacher: *One sunny day, my husband and I went fishing. I caught more fish than he did . . . One sunny day, my husband and I went fishing on Coldwater Lake. I caught ten more fish than he did . . . My husband and I like to fish on Coldwater Lake. Sometimes I catch more fish than he does.* I'm ready now.

Speak your message out loud as you write it in front of your class.

Teacher: **My husband and I like to fish on Coldwater Lake. Sometimes I catch more fish than he does.** Can you help me identify my information?

Children nod yes.

Teacher: Whom did I write about?

Student: Your husband and you.

Teacher: Could someone come up here and underline my *who* with a black marker? (*A volunteer underlines* My husband and I *in black.*) Thank you. What are we doing?

Student: Fishing.

Teacher: Could someone come up here and underline my *what* with a red marker? (*A volunteer underlines the word* fish *in red.*) Thank you. I'm pleased that I included my who and what in my message. Did I add something interesting?

Student: You wrote that sometimes you catch more fish than he does.

Teacher: Could someone come up here and underline that sentence with a green marker? (*A volunteer underlines* Sometimes I catch more fish than he does *in green.*)

Teacher: Thank you. Did I add anything else that is interesting?

Student: You wrote that you like to fish on Coldwater Lake. Coldwater Lake adds something interesting.

Teacher: Would you please come up here and underline *Coldwater Lake* in green? (*A volunteer comes forward and underlines* Coldwater Lake *in green.*) Thank you for your help. I have one last thing to check. Does my message **My husband and I like to fish on Coldwater Lake. Sometimes I catch more fish than he does** match my picture?

Children will agree that you wrote the same thing that you drew, so the words match the picture.

Teacher: Great! When you're writing in your journals this year, I'd like you to always make sure you have the who, what, and something interesting from your picture in your message.

Mini-Lesson: Finding the Who, What, and Something Interesting

~~~~~~

Place Overhead 1 (page 11) on the overhead projector. Cover samples #2 and #3. Read the first journal message of the sample #1 set out loud with expression.

Read the entry again so children become familiar with the content. Then ask these questions:

• Who is this journal message about?

• What is happening?

• Is there something interesting in the message?

Children will tell you that the who is the dog Roscoe. The what is Roscoe chasing and carrying balls. The something interesting is that the dog carries the balls back to the writer.

Literature Links

It's helpful to have a few good books that use the journal or diary format when you're speaking with children about their journal entries. Find the who, what, and something interesting in the entries in these books.

The Diary of a Worm by Doreen Cronin

The Judy Moody Mood Journal by Megan McDonald

Top-Secret Personal Beeswax: A Journal by Junie B. (and Me!) by Barbara Park

8

Read aloud the second entry with expression. Ask the above questions again. Children will tell you that the who is the dog. The what is that he chases and brings back balls. They will also tell you that is all of the information. This message contains nothing interesting.

Repeat this process for the third entry. Children will tell you that the who is the word *he*. They will be a bit miffed that the text doesn't let the reader know that it's a dog named Roscoe. The what is that he chases and brings something back, but the reader doesn't know that they are balls. The something interesting is that he brings them to the author.

Now, ask: *Which of these three journal messages has the most specific information for the who, what, and something interesting?* Children will tell you that the first entry is the strongest. It presents the name of the dog, that he chases and carries balls, and that he brings the balls back to the writer.

Finally, ask children: *How do you want to write in your journals? Like the first, second, or third entry?* Children will quickly tell you that they want to write like the first one.

Repeat the above procedure for samples #2 and #3. I suggest using only one set for a mini-lesson. Remember, mini-lessons are designed to be brief and offer children another tool to assist them in their writing.

- For sample #2, entry 1, children will answer:
  Who: *Jennifer and the writer*
  What: *they ride bikes*
  Something Interesting: *there isn't anything*

- For sample #2, entry 2, children will answer:
  Who: *the writer and her friend Jennifer*
  What: *they ride bikes around the park*
  Something Interesting: *they pedal fast, then coast downhill and around the pond*

- For sample #2, entry 3, children will answer:
  Who: *we* (It's not clear who the *we* is.)
  What: *they ride bikes fast at the park*
  Something Interesting: *they don't need to pedal around the pond*

Children will tell you that entry 2 has the most specific information. Encourage them to use that message as a model for their journal entries this year.

- For sample #3, entries 1 and 2, children will answer:
  Who: *I—the writer*
  What: *he bought something and took it home*
  Something Interesting: *the writer hung it/put it in his room*

- For sample #3, entry 3, children will answer:
  Who: *I—the writer*
  What: *he found, bought, and took home a paper sculpture of a monarch butterfly*
  Something Interesting: *it flutters above the writer's bed in his bedroom*

Children will say the third entry has the most specific information. The other two messages are vague and don't let the reader know what the writer is talking about. It's this last entry that they will enjoy the most. Encourage children to write interesting entries like this one in their own journals this year.

Reteaching Points

If children are struggling to identify the strongest journal entry, follow this procedure to help them see which information is most specific:

Ask different children to come to the overhead and underline the parts that tell who, what, and something interesting in each entry for one of the sample sets. I like to use one color to highlight the who, another color for the what, and a third color for the something interesting, as I modeled in the introductory lesson of this chapter. After they have underlined each of these three elements, children can easily compare the messages and readily identify which one has the most specific information. To further support them, ask: *Which message paints the clearest picture in your mind?*

Journal Writing: An Overview

1. Be specific with the who. Use names when possible. (*dog Roscoe, my friend Jennifer and I*)

2. Be specific with the what. (*chases and carries balls; ride bikes around the park; found, bought, and took home a paper sculpture of a monarch butterfly*)

3. Be specific with the something interesting. (*carries them back to me; we pedal fast, then coast downhill around the pond; most beautiful paper sculpture in the store; monarch butterfly with wings that glowed; it flutters above my bed in my room*)

4. Paint a clear picture in the mind of the reader by using specific information.

TIPS FOR WRITERS

How Can You Write Interesting Journal Entries?

1. First, draw a picture in your journal of what you want to write about. Make sure you draw the who, what, and at least two details.
2. Study your journal picture to decide on the who, what, and something interesting for your writing.
3. Use specific names when possible to identify the who.
4. Use specific verbs to identify the what.
5. For something interesting, tell the reader where, how, when, or why.
6. Make sure your journal message matches the journal drawing.

1

- My dog Roscoe chases balls and carries them back to me.
- My dog chases balls and brings them back.
- He chases them. He brings them to me.

2

- Jennifer and I ride bikes fast there.
- I ride bikes around the park with my friend Jennifer. We pedal fast, then coast downhill around the pond.
- We ride our bikes fast at the park. We don't need to pedal around the pond.

3

- It was the most beautiful one in the store. I bought it and took it home. It hangs in my room.
- It was pretty. I liked it and bought it. I took it home and put it in my room.
- I found the most beautiful paper sculpture in the store. It was a monarch butterfly with wings that glowed. I bought it and took it home. Now, it flutters above my bed in my room.

CHAPTER 2

Meaning

THE QUESTION TO EXPLORE

Do You Understand Everything That I've Written?

When children write what they know, care about, and feel, they are eager to get their words on paper. Everything that they write makes sense to them. Of course, they have all the background information in their minds. However, not all of that organization, detail, and language makes it into a first draft—this is true not only for student writers but also for published authors. Since we want to help these writers express themselves clearly, we need to teach them ways to confirm that all of their writing makes sense. Here is how I introduce this element of craft to children.

Introducing the Craft Element: Meaning

Before you begin, find a photograph to share that shows a person at a place that will be familiar to children. Make sure the person has a specific look on his or her face. He or she could be smiling, frowning, worried, or frightened. (The photograph that I'm using with the children shows a girl in her backyard pool. She is smiling and throwing a beach ball to her sister.)

Begin your mini-lesson on meaning like this:

Teacher: Writers share ideas, thoughts, memories, or information with an audience. It's important that the reader or audience understands what the writer is trying to say. If the meaning is interrupted or broken, the writer is not expressing himself to the reader. Let me show you what I mean. Please look at this photograph. I'm going to pretend that this picture is in my mind. I want to describe what is happening here to my audience. Help me decide what I need to write. What is happening in this picture?

Student: Two girls are in a swimming pool.

Student: One girl is smiling.

Student: That girl is throwing a ball to another girl.

Teacher: Those are some good thoughts. Tell me: where do you think this is happening?

Student: In a swimming pool.

Student: It looks like a pool in someone's backyard.

Teacher: Again, you are giving me some wonderful things to write. I'm going to write my description now. (*Read your words as you write them on chart paper in front of the children.*) **She is smiling and throwing a ball to someone.** Now, pretend you have not seen the photograph that I just showed you. Would you understand everything that I've written?

Student: You did put the part about the girl throwing a ball. I understand that.

Student: I don't know what kind of ball she's throwing.

Student: We don't know who she's throwing the ball to.

Student: We don't even know who "she" is.

Student: We don't know where all of this is happening.

Teacher: Is the meaning clear or confusing right now?

Students: Confusing.

Teacher: Let me write that description again. **My young friend Jordan is smiling and throwing a beach ball to her sister Maddie in their backyard pool.** Do you understand all of my writing now?

Student: Yes. We even know the girls' names—Jordan and Maddie.

Student: This writing is much better.

Teacher: Take another look at the photograph. Does my writing describe what you see?

Student: Yes, it does.

Student: Your writing even tells us something we can't see in the picture— their names.

Teacher: Would my writing paint this picture in the minds of my readers?

Students: Yes.

Teacher: When we have clear meaning, our audiences will know what we are writing. They will be able to see in their minds what we see or think in our minds before we write. This year we want to stop and read what we've written to make sure our meaning is clear in all of our writing. We want to make sure that our audience understands what we mean before we continue.

Mini-Lesson: Meaning

Part 1: Making Meaning in Nonfiction Writing

Place Overhead 2 (page 16) on the overhead projector. Cover the bottom two samples while you and your students examine the first piece. Read it out loud with expression for general comprehension. Read it again so children become familiar with the content. Then ask these questions:

- Do you understand everything that the author has written?
- Are there any words or sentences that seem confusing?
- Is the meaning of this piece clear to you?

Children will tell you that they understand some of the writing, but not all of it. Some children will say that the first two sentences are a bit confusing; the frogs grow into tadpoles. The rest of the piece seems to be describing the frogs. Most children will say that some of the meaning is clear, but not all.

Repeat the above process for sample #2. Children will tell you that they understand everything the author has written. Some children will mention that this one has a title and that helps the listener/reader know what the writing is about. Most children will say that there is nothing confusing about this piece. The class will agree that the meaning is clear in this one.

Repeat the process for sample #3. Children will tell you that they understand most of the writing. Having read the second sample, a few children will mention that the first sentence, *Some frogs lay eggs in water*, is a little confusing. Which frogs lay eggs in water? A few children will also mention that the last two sentences are somewhat confusing. The sentence *The tadpoles look like frogs* tells us we're still speaking about tadpoles, not frogs. So in the next sentence, when it says, *Some time, they will lay eggs in water, too*, it sounds as if the tadpoles lay the eggs. Children will say that most of the writing is clear, but not all.

Ask children: *Which piece carries the most meaning? Which one explains most clearly how tadpoles grow into frogs?* Most children will say that sample #2, "Life Cycle of a Frog," carries the most meaning. This will be the one they enjoy the most. Encourage children to write with this kind of clear meaning in their future pieces.

Part 2: Making Meaning in Fiction Writing

Place Overhead 3 (page 17) on the overhead projector. Cover the bottom sample while you and your students examine the first piece. Read it out loud with expression for general comprehension. Read it again so the children become familiar with content. Then ask these questions:

- Do you understand everything that the author has written?
- Are there any words or sentences that seem confusing?
- Is the meaning of this piece clear to you?

Children will tell you that they understand everything about this writing. They cannot find any words or sentences that are confusing, and they think the meaning is clear. Repeat the above process for the second piece. Children will tell you that it's difficult to understand much of this writing. If you ask why, they will tell you that too many of the sentences begin with *he* and *it*. Children may not know whether the author is referring to the snake or to Jerod. In the last sentence, it's unclear whether Jerod has found another snake or another trail. The class will agree that the meaning of this piece is not clear.

Ask children: *Which piece carries more meaning for you? In which one did you understand everything that the author wrote?* Children will say that the first piece carried more meaning for them. This is the one they enjoyed the most. Encourage children to write clearly like this in their own writing.

Reteaching Points

If children cannot tell you which piece carries the most meaning, or if they hesitate when deciding which piece they understood, try this: As you're examining the different pieces, have children volunteer to come up to the overhead projector and circle words or sentences that are confusing. Afterward, the class will be able to see which piece has no circles. This will be the one that they all understood.

Meaning: An Overview of the Craft Element

1. A title can often announce the topic of the writing and establish meaning. (*Life Cycle of a Frog, Surprise on the Trail*)

2. Make sure the first sentence is clear and provides the reader with basic information on the who or what. (*Female frogs lay eggs in water, Jerod walked up the mountain trail*)

3. Be specific when naming who or what is doing the action. (*tadpoles grow back legs, Jerod slowly took a step back*)

4. Use specific vocabulary throughout the writing to create meaning. (*webbed toes, shrink, mountain trail, rattlesnake, slithered*)

TIPS FOR WRITERS

What Can You Do to Make Meaning?

1. Check that your title leads the audience into your piece.
2. Read your writing out loud and ask, "Do I understand all of this writing?"
3. Read your piece to a writing friend and ask, "Do you understand all of my writing?"
4. Ask your writing friend to circle with colored pencil any words or sentences that are confusing.
5. Rewrite any confusing words or sentences so that someone else can understand everything you have written.

1

Frogs lay eggs. They grow into tadpoles. First, they have back legs. Then, they grow front legs. Their tails go away. They become frogs. One day, some of them will lay eggs.

Life Cycle of a Frog   **2**

Female frogs lay eggs in water. The eggs grow into tadpoles with tails. Soon, the tadpoles grow back legs with webbed toes. Next, they grow front legs. Finally, their tails shrink. The tadpoles are now frogs. One day, the female frogs will lay eggs.

Tadpole to Frog   **3**

Some frogs lay eggs in water. The eggs grow tails and swim away. Then, they grow back legs with webbed toes. And, they grow front legs. Later, their tails go away. The tadpoles look like frogs. Some time, they will lay eggs in water, too.

Surprise on the Trail　1

Jerod walked up the mountain trail. What a great day for a hike, he thought. A rattlesnake slithered in front of him. Jerod stopped. The snake raised its head and shook its tail. *Rattle. Rattle.* Jerod held still. The rattlesnake did not move, but it shook its tail more. Keeping his eyes on the snake, Jerod slowly took a step back. The snake remained in its spot. Jerod took another step back. The snake stopped rattling its tail. Little by little, Jerod safely inched away from the snake. Later, he found another trail and hiked for the rest of the day.

2

Jerod walked up the trail. What a great day for a hike, he thought. A snake slithered in front of him. He stopped. It raised its head and shook its tail. *Rattle. Rattle.* He held still. It did not move toward him, but it shook its tail. He watched the snake and took a small step backward. It stayed in its place.

He took another step back. It stopped rattling its tail. Little by little, he safely inched away from the snake. Later, he found another one and hiked all day long.

CHAPTER 3

Focus

Does All of My Writing Stay on My Topic?

To focus means to concentrate on one thing. When writers focus, they stay on one topic. We can help student writers focus by showing them how to create a simple plan before they write. If they think and plan around their topic, they will stay on their topic as they write.

Younger writers also enjoy going over their plans with a friend. The listeners can ask questions that can help the writers decide what they want to include, and what is unnecessary. The investment of time and thought by friends heightens the writers' commitment to the quality of their pieces.

Introducing the Craft Element: Focus

Before you ask the children to come up and sit near you for your focus mini-lesson, cut a card four inches square. In the middle of the card draw and color a large red dot. Then begin your mini-lesson on focus like this:

Teacher: Does anyone know what focus means?

Children shake their heads no.

Teacher: To focus means to concentrate on one thing. I'd like you to practice. Here is a card with a large red dot. Can everyone see it? (*Hold card up so all children can easily see it.*) I'd like you to focus on the red dot. I'm going to move the card up, down, and around, but I don't want you to take your eyes off the dot. Can you do that? Can you focus on the dot?

Children nod their heads yes.

Keep the Plan Simple

✳

In first grade, children are capable of making simple plans before they write. The purpose of the plan is to *think*. A student thinks about purpose, audience, and organization of topic. But a wonderful by-product of planning is that student writers stay focused when they have their own plans before them as they write. Here are sample plans for a piece of nonfiction and personal narrative:

Who: monarch butterfly

What: life cycle

1. lay eggs—milkweed
2. eggs hatch
3. caterpillars eat
4. spin cocoon
5. change
6. butterfly unfolds
7. beats wings

Ending: cycle begins again, never stops

Who: Dad and I

What: clean the garage

1. move car
2. take out trash
3. find lost ball
4. put things away
5. use sweeper and broom

Ending: Mom happy, ice cream for us

Try to avoid the use of ready-made graphic organizers. Encourage children to make their own plans that fit their writing. When the plan is organic, children are much more likely to use it.

Teacher: Remember, keep your eyes on the dot—focus. (*Move the card slowly up, down, diagonally, and around in a circle.*) Excellent. Everyone kept their eyes on the dot. All of your attention was focused on the red dot. Writers need to focus, too. Can you tell me how a writer would focus?

Student: He keeps his eyes on his writing.

Student: He only thinks about his writing.

Teacher: Both of those are good thoughts and are definitely part of how a writer focuses. What if I said that a writer focuses on his topic, on what he wants to say? How would a writer focus on his topic?

Student: He would only think about his topic.

Student: The only things he would write would be about his topic.

Teacher: You're absolutely correct. When a writer focuses, he thinks about his topic. It's like his mind can only think about that one thing. When he writes, all of his sentences stay on his topic. This year when we write, I hope that we think about our topic and make sure that all of our writing stays on that topic.

Mini-lesson: Focus

Part 1: Staying on Topic in Narrative Writing

Place Overhead 4 (page 23) on the overhead projector. Cover the bottom sample while you and your students examine the top piece. Read it out loud with expression for general comprehension. Read it again so children become familiar with the content. Then ask these questions:

- What is the author writing about? What is the topic?
- Does everything in this piece of writing stay on that topic?
- Are there any words or sentences that take the reader away from the topic?
- Are there any words or sentences that need to be removed from this piece so that it is focused?

Children will tell you that the topic of the first "Snowy Wonderland" sample is how a snowfall can make a backyard more beautiful. They will say that not everything in this piece of writing stays on that topic. The words or sentences that take the reader away from the topic are

> *I've read about them in stories.*
>
> *Have you?*
>
> *Some people think ice cream or new shoes are special.*
>
> *Not me, I like snow.*
>
> *. . . just like the small cotton balls in your bathroom.*

After children have listed or crossed out words or sentences that take the reader away from the focus, reread the piece, omitting these parts. Ask children: *Is all the writing now focused on the topic?*

Repeat the process for sample #2. Children will tell you that the topic of the second piece is how a snowfall can change a backyard into something beautiful.

Find the Focus

If children seem to be having a difficult time identifying the words or sentences that take the reader from the focus, read each sentence again, one at a time. Ask children: Do all of these words and thoughts talk about a snowy wonderland? If the answer is no, ask a child to come to the overhead projector and draw a line through the words or sentences that do not stay on the focus of the piece. This exercise will provide a graphic that will help children "see" the extraneous information or ideas.

They will say that all of this writing stays on the topic. It is a focused piece of writing. They will not find any words or sentences that take the reader away from the focus; therefore there is nothing to remove. But if the children are not sure, go back and reread each sentence, one at a time, and ask them whether that sentence remains on the topic.

After reading both versions of "Snowy Wonderland," ask children: *Which piece is more focused? Does all the writing stay on the topic?* Children will announce that the second piece is more focused. This is the sample that they will enjoy the most. Encourage children to stay as focused in their writing as the author did in sample #2.

Part 2: Staying on Topic in Nonfiction

Place Overhead 5 (page 24) on the overhead projector. Cover the bottom sample while you and your class examine the piece at the top of the page. Read it out loud with expression for general comprehension. Read it again so children become familiar with content. Then ask these questions:

- What is the author writing about? What is the topic?

- Does everything in this piece of writing stay on that topic?

- Are there any words or sentences that take the reader away from the topic?

- Are there any words or sentences that need to be removed from this piece so that it is focused?

Children will tell you that this piece of writing is about young leopards. If you ask them how they know that, they will tell you that the title is "Young Leopards" and all the information is about young leopards. Children will say that everything in this paragraph stays on that topic. They'll find that there are no words or sentences that take the reader away from the topic. Nothing needs to be removed to improve the focus of this piece. Repeat this process for sample #2 at the bottom of the page. Children will tell you that the topic is the same—young leopards. However, they will not think that everything in this piece stays on the topic. They may offer these words or sentences that take the reader away from the topic:

> *They are not like house cats that have litters of five or more kittens.*
> *But cubs are not as tame as kittens.*
> *Someone won't be pouring their dinner into food bowls.*

To remove these from the text, ask volunteers to come to the overhead projector and draw lines through the unnecessary phrases or sentences. Then, reread the piece and see if it is more focused than before.

Ask children: *Which piece is more focused? Does all the writing stay on topic?* Children will announce that sample #1 is more focused. This is the sample that they will enjoy the most. Encourage children to write with focus.

Reteaching Points

If children hesitate or cannot tell you which fiction sample from Overhead 4 is more focused, place that transparency back on the overhead projector. Show both samples at the same time. Ask children: *In which piece did the author write only about the snowy wonderland? In which piece did the author add extra details that do not tell us more about the snowy wonderland?*

If children have not drawn lines through the unnecessary words or sentences, help them do that now. This will help them see which piece is more focused.

Repeat the process for the nonfiction samples from Overhead 5. Ask children: *In which piece did the author write only about young leopards? In which piece did the author add extra information that takes the reader away from the topic of young leopards?* Again, if children have not drawn lines through the unnecessary words or sentences, help them do that now. They will soon see which piece is more focused.

Focus: An Overview of the Craft Element

1. The title often announces the topic. (*Snowy Wonderland, Young Leopards*)

2. The lead of the first sentence or two usually states the focus. (*A new snowfall is like a magic wand, It changes everyday things in my backyard into objects of beauty, Female leopards give birth to two or three baby cubs at a time*)

3. Each sentence adds more meaning to the topic.

TIPS FOR WRITERS

What Can You Do to Stay on Topic?

1. Make a brief plan before you write to focus ideas and information.
2. Name the topic of your writing.
3. Create a title that tells about the topic of the writing.
4. Make sure your lead sentence states the topic of your writing.
5. Read each sentence of your writing and ask yourself, *Does this add meaning to my topic?*
6. Ask a writing friend to listen to your piece and check if all the sentences stay on your topic.
7. You or a writing friend can cross out any words or sentences that are not focused on the topic.
8. Rewrite your piece, removing any unnecessary words or sentences.

Snowy Wonderland ①

A new snowfall is like a magic wand. I've read about them in stories. Have you? A magic wand can change everyday things into objects of beauty. Some people think ice cream or new shoes are special. Not me—I like snow. Snow changes regular bushes into giant cotton balls. They're fluffy and white, just like the small cotton balls in your bathroom. Snow makes my birdbath become a white mushroom that grows taller and taller. It turns the garage into an icy castle sparkling overhead. I always think of castles when my backyard is a snowy wonderland.

Snowy Wonderland ②

A new snowfall is like a magic wand. It changes everyday things in my backyard into objects of beauty. Snow-covered bushes become giant cotton balls. My birdbath is a crystal mushroom growing taller and taller with each snowflake. A new snowfall turns my garage into an icy castle sparkling overhead. My backyard becomes a winter wonderland just for me!

Young Leopards   1

Female leopards give birth to two or three baby cubs at a time. Cubs weigh about one pound at birth and look like spotted kittens. Cubs must learn how to hunt. At first, they chase and catch mice and rabbits. Later, they learn how to catch bigger animals like deer.

Young Leopards   2

Female leopards give birth to two or three baby cubs at a time. They are not like house cats that have litters of five or more kittens. Cubs weigh about one pound and look like kittens. But cubs are not as tame as kittens. Cubs must learn how to hunt. Someone won't be pouring their dinner into food bowls. At first they chase and catch small animals because they are small, too. Later they will catch bigger animals.

CHAPTER 4

Organization

Does My Writing Have a B, M, M, M, E?

Young writers understand order and organization. They know that teachers introduce topics with interesting details when they want to engage them in learning. Storytellers introduce characters and problems at the beginning of their picture books, a structure that children learn from the many books they listen to and read each day. Children expect action and suspense to build through a series of events in stories. They've seen this happen again and again in the cartoons, TV shows, and movies that they watch. First-grade writers know that by the end of a story they usually know how everything turns out. They remember that feeling of satisfaction at the end of a narrative. Little by little, student writers have been learning the structure or organization of fiction and information writing. Our job is to show them how to write with the same well-ordered approach they have come to expect in their reading. We can teach them ways to organize their thoughts in their heads and on paper before they write.

Introducing the Craft Element: Organization

Begin your mini-lesson on organization like this:

Teacher: How many of you like to build your own outdoor tents from sheets?

Some children raise hands.

Teacher: Tell me what it looks like when your tent is completed.

Student: It looks like a big white tent outside under the trees with a place where we can crawl in.

Student: We tie a bunch of sheets together and it looks like a big, long tunnel. We go in the one end and set up different rooms inside.

Teacher: So when you decide you want an outside tent, does it happen all at once?

Student: No, it takes us the whole morning to build the thing.

Teacher: What do you do first?

Student: We ask Mom or Dad for sheets to use.

Student: We carry out chairs and collect poles to hold up the sheets.

Student: We get everything we need together first, then we build it.

Teacher: So to make an outside tent from sheets, you collect your materials and then build your tent. Do I understand you correctly?

Children nod yes.

Teacher: Have you ever just taken sheets outside and tried to make a tent without chairs or poles?

Children laugh.

Student: That wouldn't work. What would make the sheets stay up? I mean, you can use a skinny tree for one corner, but what would hold up the rest of the sheet?

Teacher: So to make a whole tent, or a tent of rooms, you need to do things in a certain order. You need to put parts together in a certain way. Is that right? (*Children nod heads yes.*) Can you tell me what you do first, second, third, and fourth to make a tent?

Student: Sure. First we collect everything we need: sheets, poles, chairs, and sometimes string or yarn.

Student: Then you put your chairs or poles out in the yard and you hook your sheets to them. This can take a long time because they can come apart.

Student: Yeah, getting it to stay together is the hardest part.

Teacher: After that, what do you do?

Student: You make a place where you can go inside. It needs to be a place where you can move the sheet back and it won't make the whole tent fall down.

Student: Then comes the fun part. We take water and juice and snacks and books and games into the tent. We stay out there all day in our own secret world.

Teacher: So let me review everything you've said. You organize your materials to build the tent first. You carefully build your tent. After that, you turn your tent into a fun place where you can eat and read and play games. Does that sound correct?

Students: Yes. You've got it. That's what we do.

Teacher: You have just described the organization needed to build a backyard tent. Authors need organization to build clear writing, too. Just like tent builders, they do some things at the beginning, in the middle, and at the end of their writing. Authors think about what they want to write and how to write it. Then they put their parts together one at a time until they have created a whole piece of writing that makes sense to an audience. This year we are going to study many pieces of writing to learn how writers organize their thoughts and sentences. I would like you to remember that all writing has a beginning, at least three middle parts, and an end. Let's learn what each of these parts does.

Mini-Lesson: Organization

Part 1: Organizing a Personal Narrative

Place Overhead 6 (page 34) on the overhead projector. Cover the bottom samples while you and your class examine the first sample. Read it out loud with expression for general comprehension. Read it again so children become familiar with the content. Then ask these questions, one at a time, and give children time to respond to each one before moving on to the next:

- Does this piece have a beginning? A beginning introduces the topic or the character of the piece. It usually is the first one or two sentences.
- Does this piece have a middle? The middle usually has three or more details or pieces of information or events (things that happen).
- Does this piece have an ending? An ending is usually a sentence or two that pulls the story or nonfiction piece to a close. An ending satisfies the reader.

Children will tell you that sample #1 does have a beginning: *Yesterday, my dog Samson and I played at Shoaff Park*. They will say that there is a little bit of a middle: *we chased each other around the swings and over the bridge*. But there are not three events or happenings in this middle. They will also tell you that it does have an ending: *After a spin on the merry-go-round, Samson and I hurried home, hungry for lunch*.

You may want to ask children if this is a well-organized piece of writing with a fully developed beginning, middle, middle, middle, and end (B, M, M, M, E). Most children will tell you that it has those parts but is not fully developed.

Show them sample #2 on the overhead projector. Read it out loud with expression for general comprehension. Read it again so children become familiar with the content. Then ask the questions above, one at a time. Children will tell you that this piece does have a beginning: *Yesterday, my dog Samson and I played at Shoaff Park*. They will also tell you that this piece has a middle with five to six actions, including

> *we chased each other around the swings and over the bridge*
>
> *we curled up in the sun and rested*
>
> *a squirrel ran by*

the squirrel tried to hide and Samson was on the hunt

the squirrel finally found its nest

Children will tell you that this piece also has an ending: *After a spin on the merry-go-round, Samson and I hurried home, hungry for lunch.* If you ask children if this piece is organized with a fully developed beginning, middle, and end, they will tell you that it is.

Place the third sample of "Excitement in the Park" on the overhead projector. Read it out loud with expression for general comprehension. Read it again so children become familiar with the content. Then, ask the questions listed above, one at a time. Children will tell you that this piece has no beginning. The reader doesn't know who "us" is and what tuckered "us" out. Children will say that the piece has some middle actions:

we curled up in the sun and rested

a squirrel ran by

the squirrel tried to hide and Samson was on the hunt

the squirrel finally found its nest, and we never saw it again

Plans Are Great Organizers!

This plan shows how you can help children find the three organizational parts of their writing.

(B) Who: Grandma and I

(B) What: bake cookies

(M) Details:

1. find recipe	4. mix
2. get ingredients	5. shape cookies
3. measure	6. bake in oven

(E) Ending: invite friends—eat cookies and play games

After children have created a plan, have them draw boxes or circles around each of the organizational parts and label them. For a personal narrative, the who and what belong in the beginning, or lead, of the piece. The details form the middle, and the ending comes at the end, of course.

Having this organizational scheme in front of them helps student writers know what they're writing at each point in their piece. They can look at their plans and decide whether they have enough events or details in the middle. They feel confident because they can work toward a satisfying ending. Some children also enjoy checking off each part as they add it to their writing. It gives them a sense of accomplishment.

Children will tell you that this piece has the same ending as the other pieces: *After a spin on the merry-go-round, Samson and I hurried home, hungry for lunch.*

After reading and discussing each sample from Overhead 6, place the transparency back on the overhead projector, showing all three pieces at once. Ask: *Which piece is the best organized? Which one has a fully developed beginning, middle, middle, middle, and end?* Children will tell you that sample #2 is the best organized. This is the sample that they will enjoy the most. Encourage children to organize their writing this year, either with their plans or by checking for all three parts.

Part 2: Organizing a Story

Place Overhead 7 (page 35) on the overhead projector. Cover the bottom samples while you and your class examine the piece at the top of the page. Read it out loud with expression for general comprehension.

Read it aloud a second time so children become familiar with the content. Then ask these questions, one at a time, waiting for responses to each one before asking the next:

- Does this piece have a beginning? A beginning introduces the topic or the character of the piece. It usually is the first one or two sentences.

- Does this piece have a middle? The middle usually has three or more details or pieces of information or events (things that happen).

- Does this piece have an ending? An ending is usually a sentence or two that pulls the story or nonfiction piece to a close. An ending satisfies the reader.

Children will tell you that this piece has a beginning. It begins with *BRRRRNNGGGG!* and ends with *It wasn't there!* They will say that the only middle action is *Maddie shut her eyes and took several deep breaths.*

Prompt them further: *Is one middle action enough to develop the story? Do we really see Maddie struggle with only one middle action?* Children will tell you that one action is not enough to make a middle of a story. Authors try to have three or more middle actions to build tension and engage the reader. The class will agree that sample #1 has a good ending starting with *"That's it!" she said out loud* and ending with *Maddie slid her sister's treasure into her pocket and hurried down the hall to her bus.*

Repeat the above process with sample #2. Children will say that sample #2 has no beginning. The reader is thrown immediately into Maddie's struggle. They can identify these three middle actions:

Maddie reached up and ran her hand all over the shelf.

She raced back into the classroom and searched in her desk.

"Maddie," said her teacher. "You'd better hurry or you'll miss your bus."

Remind children that without a beginning, these middle actions do not carry much meaning for the reader. Finally, children will say that there is a quick ending for sample #2: *Maddie thought for a moment and found the necklace.*

If you ask children, *Is this a well-developed story with a B, M, M, M, and E?*, they will answer no. There is no beginning, an OK middle, and a quick ending.

Repeat this reading and questioning process for sample #3. Children will tell you that sample #3 has a strong beginning, starting with *BRRRRNNGGGG!* and ending with *It wasn't there!* They will say that there is a complete middle with these actions:

> *She reached up and ran her hand all over the shelf.*
>
> *Maddie looked in her book bag.*
>
> *She raced back into the classroom and searched in her desk.*
>
> *"Maddie," said her teacher. "You'd better hurry or you'll miss your bus."*
>
> *Stop, she thought. Calm down.*
>
> *Maddie shut her eyes and took a deep breath.*

Children will then tell you that there is a developed ending that begins with *"That's it!" she said out loud* and ends with *Maddie slid her sister's treasure into her pocket and hurried down the hall to her bus.*

Ask children: *Is this an organized story? Does it have a well-developed beginning, middle, middle, middle, and end?* Children will quickly say that this is an organized and well-developed story.

Now, place the transparency with all three samples of "Uh-Oh!" showing on the overhead projector. Ask children: *Which of these sample stories is the best organized?* The children will say that sample #3 is the best-organized story. They can identify all three organizational parts of the story. This is the sample they will enjoy the most. Encourage children to either organize their stories in their plans or check for the B, M, M, M, and E in their written work.

Part 3: Organizing Nonfiction Writing

Place Overhead 8 (page 36) on the overhead projector. Cover the bottom samples while you and your students examine sample #1 at the top of the page. Read it out loud with expression for general comprehension. Read it again so children become familiar with the content. Then ask these questions, one at a time, waiting for a response to one question before continuing on to the next:

- Does this piece have a beginning? A beginning introduces the topic or the character of the piece. It usually is the first one or two sentences.
- Does this piece have a middle? The middle usually has three or more details or pieces of information or events (things that happen).
- Does this piece have an ending? An ending is usually a sentence or two that pulls the story or nonfiction piece to a close. An ending satisfies the reader.

Children will tell you that sample #1 does have a beginning, which introduces the topic of amphibians. It begins with *Amphibians are animals that can live both on land and in water.* They will say that this nonfiction piece does have a middle, which has these pieces of information:

> *Frogs, toads, and salamanders are all amphibians.*

Amphibians use gills to breathe underwater and lungs to breathe on land.

Amphibians have mucus on their skin.

The mucus keeps their skin moist.

Sometimes it [mucus] protects them from enemies.

Children can identify an ending. It begins with *These are some of the features of amphibians. Have you ever seen one in the wild?*

Ask children: *Does this piece have a well-developed beginning, middle, middle, middle, and end?* They will tell you that it does.

Repeat the process with sample #2. Children will tell you that sample #2 does have a beginning: *Amphibians are animals that can live both on land and in water.* They will list these as the middle pieces of information:

Frogs, toads, and salamanders are all amphibians.

Amphibians use gills to breathe underwater and lungs to breathe on land.

Ask children: *Is this a well-developed middle of three or more pieces of information?* Most children will say that it is not well developed, that they expect more information in the middle. Children will say that sample #2 has no ending. The reader is left dangling. There is no reader satisfaction.

Follow up with these questions: *Is this an organized piece of writing? Does it have a beginning, middle, middle, middle, and end?* Children will decide that this is not an organized piece of writing. It does not have all the parts to create a whole.

Repeat the process with sample #3. Children will say that this piece has no beginning. They will tell you that the middle pieces of information are

Amphibians use gills to breathe underwater and lungs to breathe on land.

Amphibians have mucus on their skin.

The mucus keeps their skin moist and sometimes it protects them from enemies.

Children will also note that this piece has no ending. Actually it is simply a list of facts.

Ask children to evaluate: *Is this an organized piece of writing? Does it have a beginning, middle, middle, middle, and end?* They will say that this sample is not organized. There is no beginning or ending.

Now, display all three nonfiction pieces from Overhead 8 at once. Ask children: *Which sample of nonfiction is the most organized?* Children will agree that sample #1 is the most organized. It contains all three organizational parts: beginning, middle, and end. This is the sample that they will enjoy the most. Encourage children to always check that they have a beginning, middle, middle, middle, and end in their nonfiction writing.

Reteaching Points

If children hesitate or cannot tell you which sample in a set is most organized, revisit the samples and ask children to underline or highlight the beginnings in red, the middles in black, and the endings in blue. Then go back and look for

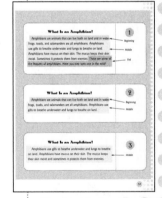

The highlighted sections on page 33 show which version of the nonfiction paragraph "What Is an Amphibian?" has a complete B, M, M, M, E structure.

evidence of all three colors in each piece. This provides children with an additional graphic support to identify beginnings, middles, and ends. You may also want to use page 33 as a reproducible or overhead transparency to highlight the structure of three nonfiction pieces.

Organization: An Overview of the Craft Element

1. A brief plan helps writers organize their writing before they begin. A simple plan for "What Is an Amphibian?" might look like this:

    B: *what—amphibians—live on land and in water*
    M: *name some amphibians*
    M: *gills and lungs*
    M: *mucus*
    M: *mucus—skin*
    M: *mucus—protect*
    E: *reader—have you seen one?*

2. The beginning introduces the topic or character to the reader. (*Amphibians are animals that can live both on land and in water.*)

3. The middle provides the reader with three or more details, pieces of information, or events. (*Frogs, toads, and salamanders are all amphibians; Amphibians have mucus on their skin; Amphibians use gills to breathe underwater and lungs to breathe on land.*)

4. The ending pulls the story or nonfiction piece to a close. It satisfies the reader. (*These are some of the features of amphibians. Have you ever seen one in the wild?*)

5. A well-organized piece of writing needs to have all three of these organizational parts.

TIPS FOR WRITERS

What Can You Do to Organize Your Writing?

1. Make a brief plan before you write to organize your ideas and information.
2. Find the beginning in your writing and mark it with a *B*. Find the three or more middle details and mark each with an *M*. Find the ending of your piece and mark it with an *E*.
3. Ask a writer friend to identify your beginning. Does it pull the reader into your topic or story?
4. Ask a writer friend to help you underline three middle details, pieces of information, or events (things that happen).
5. Ask a writer friend to find your ending. Does it pull the story or nonfiction piece to a close? Does your friend feel satisfied?

What Is an Amphibian?

Amphibians are animals that can live both on land and in water. — *Beginning*

Frogs, toads, and salamanders are all amphibians. Amphibians use gills to breathe underwater and lungs to breathe on land. — *Middle*

Amphibians have mucus on their skin. The mucus keeps their skin moist. Sometimes it protects them from enemies. These are some of the features of amphibians. Have you ever seen one in the wild? — *End*

1

What Is an Amphibian?

Amphibians are animals that can live both on land and in water. — *Beginning*

Frogs, toads, and salamanders are all amphibians. Amphibians use gills to breathe underwater and lungs to breathe on land. — *Middle*

2

What Is an Amphibian?

Amphibians use gills to breathe underwater and lungs to breathe on land. Amphibians have mucus on their skin. The mucus keeps their skin moist and sometimes it protects them from enemies. — *Middle*

3

Excitement at the Park 1

Yesterday, my dog Samson and I played at Shoaff Park. At first, we chased each other around the swings and over the bridge. After a spin on the merry-go-round, Samson and I hurried home, hungry for lunch.

Excitement at the Park 2

Yesterday, my dog Samson and I played at Shoaff Park. At first, we chased each other around the swings and over the bridge. That tuckered us out, so we curled up in the sun and rested until . . . a squirrel ran by. From that point on, the game was hide-and-seek. The squirrel tried to hide and Samson was on the hunt. The squirrel finally found its nest, and we never saw it again. After a spin on the merry-go-round, Samson and I hurried home, hungry for lunch.

Excitement at the Park 3

That tuckered us out, so we curled up in the sun and rested until . . . a squirrel ran by. From that point on, the game was hide-and-seek. The squirrel tried to hide and Samson was on the hunt. The squirrel finally found its nest, and we never saw it again. After a spin on the merry-go-round, Samson and I hurried home, hungry for lunch.

Uh-Oh!   1

BRRRRNNGGGG! *Time to go home*, thought Maddie. She opened her school locker to get her books and her sister Jordan's gold necklace. (Maddie had borrowed it without asking.) It wasn't there! Maddie shut her eyes and took several deep breaths. "That's it!" she said out loud. Maddie remembered showing the necklace to her best friend, Grace, after gym. She'd been in a rush and placed the necklace in one of her gym shoes for safekeeping. Maddie reached inside her shoe. The necklace! Maddie slid her sister's treasure into her pocket and hurried down the hall to her bus.

Uh-Oh!   2

Maddie reached up and ran her hand all over the shelf. No necklace! She raced back into the classroom and searched in her desk. No necklace! "Maddie," said her teacher. "You'd better hurry or you'll miss your bus." Maddie thought for a moment and found the necklace.

Uh-Oh!   3

BRRRRNNGGGG! *Time to go home*, thought Maddie. She opened her school locker to get her books and the gold necklace she had borrowed from her sister Jordan. It wasn't there! She reached up and ran her hand all over the shelf. No necklace! Classmates filed past her on their way to the buses. Maddie looked in her book bag. No necklace! She raced back into the classroom and searched in her desk. No necklace!

"Maddie," said her teacher. "You'd better hurry or you'll miss your bus."

Maddie knew she couldn't go home without the necklace. Her heart was exploding in her chest. *Stop*, she thought. *Calm down*. Maddie shut her eyes and took a deep breath. "That's it!" she said out loud. Maddie remembered showing the necklace to her best friend, Grace, after gym. She'd placed the necklace in one of her gym shoes for safekeeping. Maddie rushed to her locker and reached inside her shoe. The necklace! Maddie slid her sister's treasure into her pocket and hurried down the hall to her bus.

What Is an Amphibian? 1

Amphibians are animals that can live both on land and in water. Frogs, toads, and salamanders are all amphibians. Amphibians use gills to breathe underwater and lungs to breathe on land. Amphibians have mucus on their skin. The mucus keeps their skin moist. Sometimes it protects them from enemies. These are some of the features of amphibians. Have you ever seen one in the wild?

What Is an Amphibian? 2

Amphibians are animals that can live both on land and in water. Frogs, toads, and salamanders are all amphibians. Amphibians use gills to breathe underwater and lungs to breathe on land.

What Is an Amphibian? 3

Amphibians use gills to breathe underwater and lungs to breathe on land. Amphibians have mucus on their skin. The mucus keeps their skin moist and sometimes it protects them from enemies.

CHAPTER 5

Vocabulary

Do My Words Paint a Picture?

Writers love words, especially when they can find just the right ones to paint pictures in the minds of their readers. Specific vocabulary is a powerful tool. Student authors recognize this and enjoy learning how to identify and use specific nouns and strong verbs in their writing. Whenever I introduce new vocabulary to children I tell them, "I'm presenting you with a gift that will last a lifetime." Do that for your students. Teach them to value and appreciate thoughtful word choice. With this craft tool, they will be able to articulate their ideas, stories, information, and feelings for years to come.

Introducing the Craft Element: Vocabulary

Begin your mini-lesson on vocabulary like this:

Teacher: Please shut your eyes and think of what you see when I say the word *plant*. What do you see in your mind?

Answers will vary from *tomato* to *rose* to *weed* to *flower* to *tree* to *vine*.

Teacher: Now shut your eyes again and think of what you see when I say the word *sunflower*.

Most children will describe the shape and colors of a sunflower. They will use words like *big, tall, bright yellow, lots of seeds, round and big, big stalk*, and *pretty flower*.

Teacher: Which word was more specific? Which one painted a more detailed picture in your mind? *Plant* or *sunflower*?

Children will tell you that when they heard the word *sunflower* they all saw about the same thing in their mind. So *sunflower* painted a more detailed picture.

Teacher: Let's do that one more time. Please shut your eyes and think of what you see when I say the word *tree*.

Answers will vary from *tall oak tree* to *evergreen tree* to *Christmas tree* to *dead tree* to *apple tree* to *walnut tree*.

Teacher: Thank you. I'd like one of you to think of a specific tree that you could name—that you think would paint almost the same detailed picture in all of our minds. When you have a tree name, raise your hand, please.

Student: I'd like everyone to tell me what they see in their minds when I say *pine tree*.

Teacher: OK, everyone, describe what you see.

Student answers may include *green needles, branches full of needles, pine-cones, needles blowing in the wind, a tall green tree*, and *a Christmas tree without lights*.

Teacher: Great job. Which one was more specific? *Tree* or *pine tree*?

Students: *Pine tree*.

Teacher: Yes. This year as writers, we always want to stop and think of the words that will paint the clearest pictures for our readers. We want to be specific for our audience.

If you would like to repeat this mini-lesson on another day, here are some pairs of words that work well with younger children: *boy* and *prince*; *paper* and *gift wrap*; *walked* and *limped*; *street* and *highway*; *food* and *watermelon*.

Remind children that whenever they take the time to make a thoughtful word choice, they are adding more meaning to their writing. The more specific the pictures, the better the reader understands the writing.

Mini-Lesson: Vocabulary

Part 1: Choosing the Right Words

Place Overhead 9 (page 43) on the overhead projector. Cover the bottom sample while you and your class examine sample #1. Read it out loud with expression for general comprehension. Read it again so children become familiar with content. Then ask:

• Which words or groups of words paint clear pictures in your mind?

On the transparency, circle these words as children call them out, encouraging children to look at nouns (names of people, places, or things) and verbs (action words). In sample #1, children will find these words, or some of these words, that paint clear pictures:

> *grandmother's face*
>
> *hard work and love*

skin is dark

hanging clothes and picking vegetables

teeth are a little yellow

dimples

smile and laugh

- Are there any words that are too general, that don't paint any pictures?

Underline these words on the transparency as children call them out. Children will notice that these descriptions, or some of these words, are too general.

Her eyes

many books

all the stuff

for the people in her life

Uncover sample #2 on Overhead 9 and repeat the process from above. Children will identify these words, or some of these words, that paint clear pictures:

grandmother's face	*picking vegetables in the summer heat*
portrait of hard work and love	*teeth are a little yellow*
blue eyes, almost gray now	*sampling homemade soups, jellies, and frosting*
show the hours she spent reading to her children and grandchildren	*for more than 75 years*
darkened skin	*dimples*
reflects months	*paint her true personality*
hanging clothes	*smile and a hearty laugh*
	family and friends in her life

Children will have a difficult time finding words that are too general, that do not help paint pictures. You might want to count and compare the number of circled words in sample #1 and sample #2.

After reading and discussing these two pieces of writing, place both on the overhead projector and ask: *Which piece shows more thoughtful word choice? Which one paints more pictures?* Children will tell you that sample #2 shows more thoughtful word choice—that it paints more pictures. This will be the piece that they enjoy. They will try to model their writing after this piece. I always enjoy asking children which word or phrase they think really adds spark to this piece of writing. Favorites are usually *portrait, sampling,* and *hearty laugh.* I think it's important to ask this because, inevitably, if a child mentions a word, he or she will try to incorporate that word into his or her own writing in the near future.

Part 2: More Practice With Word Choice

Place Overhead 10 (page 44) on the overhead projector. Cover the bottom sample while you and your students examine sample #1. Read it out loud with expression for general comprehension. Read it again so children become familiar with the content. Then ask:

- Which words or groups of words paint clear pictures in your mind? On the transparency, circle these words as children call them out, encouraging children to look at nouns (names of people, places, or things) and verbs (action words). In sample #1, children will identify these words, or some of these words, that paint clear pictures:

  small rabbit

  snuggled deep

  tall grass

  bunny lay

  nest padded

  dry brush

  tufts of fur

  round body

  no bigger than a fist

  long ears

  stretched flat

  across its back

  rested still as a stone

  body rise and fall with every breath

  slinked away

  natural hideaway

It will be difficult for children to find words that are too general or don't paint pictures.

Uncover sample #2. Repeat the process described above. Children will identify these words, or some of these words, that paint clear pictures:

  small rabbit

  tall grass

  dried plants

  long ears

Underline words children find that are too general or that do not paint pictures, including *sitting*

it was in a nest

really small

didn't move

I walked away

Again, you may want to ask children to count the circled words on sample #1 and on sample #2 for a quick comparison.

After reading and discussing these two pieces of writing, place both on the overhead projector and ask the children: *Which piece shows more thoughtful word choice? Which one paints more pictures?* Children will announce that sample #1, "Safe Hideaway," shows more thoughtful word choice, that it paints more pictures. Again, ask the children which word or group of words really caught their attention or added interest to the piece. Some of the usual responses are *snuggled deep, tufts of fur,* and *rested still as a stone.* Look for these words to pop up in their writing. What children value, they use.

Reteaching Points

If children hesitate or cannot tell you which sample in a set shows more thoughtful word choice, take a pair of samples and follow this example:

Teacher: I have made lists of both the specific words and the general words that you found in these pieces. Would someone like to select one image from the thoughtful word choice list?

Student: *Teeth are a little yellow.*

Teacher: Can you draw what that means? Do you have enough information to make a picture?

Children will tell you yes.

Teacher: Brian, I'd like you to draw that image for us while we go on, please. Could someone select one image from the too-general list?

Student: *All the stuff.*

Teacher: Can you draw this? Do you have enough information to make a picture?

Student: We could try, but none of our pictures would be the same.

Teacher: Why?

Student: Because *stuff* could be a lot of different things.

Teacher: I see. The word choice does not help you see a picture.

Repeat this process for one or two more images from both lists. Then show children the transparency of the samples with the specific words circled or underlined, and ask which piece has more images that could be drawn or acted out. This will be the sample with the more thoughtful word choice.

Literature Links

For another mini-lesson, read selected pages from one of these books to children and ask them to listen for words or groups of words that paint pictures (you may choose to keep a written record on display of those words or phrases that appeal to them):

Davy Crockett Saves the World by Rosalyn Schanzer

Flicker Flash by Joan Bransfield Graham

Weaving the Rainbow by George Ella Lyon

When Marian Sang by Pam Munoz Ryan

Vocabulary: An Overview of the Craft Element

1. Use specific names of people, places, and things (nouns) when you write.

    *   Instead of writing *friend*, use the name of your friend—*Corey*.
    *   Instead of writing *the lake*, use the name of the lake—*Clear Lake*.
    *   Instead of writing *the tool*, use the name of the tool—*hammer*.

2. Use specific verbs to tell us how something moved or what it did.

    *   Instead of writing *went*, use *bicycled*.
    *   Instead of writing *touched*, use *patted*.
    *   Instead of writing *flew*, use *soared*.

3. Use comparisons to show the size, shape, or color of an object or animal. Instead of writing *her hair was gold*, write *her hair was the color of a candle flame*. Instead of writing *the caterpillar was small*, write *a caterpillar the size of an eyelash*. Instead of writing *the ribbon was skinny*, write *the ribbon looped around her finger like spaghetti*.

TIPS FOR WRITERS

What Can You Do to Paint Pictures With Words?

1. Use specific nouns and verbs in your plan.
2. Use a dictionary or thesaurus to find more specific words.
3. Read one sentence at a time from your writing and ask, "Can I use more specific words?"
4. Ask a writing friend to read your writing and find words that paint pictures in his or her mind.
5. Read your writing and look for one weak word that you can change to a more thoughtful word.

My Grandmother's Face 1

My grandmother's face shows hard work and love. Her eyes have read many books to children. Her skin is dark from hanging clothes and picking vegetables in the hot sun. Her teeth are a little yellow from tasting all the stuff she made in her kitchen each year. But it's her dimples that show the real her. She always has a smile and laugh for the people in her life.

My Grandmother's Face 2

My grandmother's face is a portrait of hard work and love. Her blue eyes, almost gray now, show the hours she spent reading to her children and grandchildren. Her darkened skin reflects months of hanging clothes and picking vegetables in the summer heat. Her teeth are a little yellow from sampling homemade soups, jellies, and frosting for more than 75 years. But it's her dimples that paint her true personality. My grandmother always has a smile and a hearty laugh for the family and friends in her life.

Safe Hideaway   1

I found a small rabbit snuggled deep in tall grass. The bunny lay in a nest padded with dry brush and tufts of fur. Its round body was no bigger than a fist. Long ears stretched flat across its back. Even though the bunny rested still as a stone, I could see its body rise and fall with every breath. I slinked away, hoping the natural hideaway would keep the rabbit safe.

Safe Place   2

I saw a small rabbit sitting in the tall grass. It was in a nest made of dried plants and fur. Its body was really small. Its long ears were across most of its back. The bunny didn't move, but I could see it breathing. I walked away, hoping that place would keep the rabbit safe.

CHAPTER 6

Details

Is My Writing Interesting?

Details are the interesting pieces of information that add pizzazz, authenticity, and honesty to a piece of writing. Writers can use details to help describe a setting, the way Libba Moore Gray does at the beginning of *Miss Tizzy* when she writes, "Miss Tizzy's house was pink and sat like a fat blossom in the middle of a street with white houses, white fences, and very neat flower gardens." Details can also help introduce a character. In *Night Noises* by Mem Fox we learn that Lily Laceby's hair was "as wispy as cobwebs in ceilings. Her bones were as creaky as floorboards at midnight." Details can make a reader feel nervous or sad. In *Charlotte's Web* by E. B. White, our hearts tear a little with Wilbur as Charlotte's children balloon away: "The air was now so full of balloonists that the barn cellar looked almost as though a mist had gathered. Balloons by the dozen were rising, circling, and drifting away through the door, sailing off on the gentle wind. Cries of 'Good-bye, good-bye, good-bye!' came weakly to Wilbur's ears."

As we help student writers identify details in published work, they will begin to add details to their own narratives and nonfiction. No one enjoys lifeless, uninteresting writing. Children are eager to include interesting information that makes their writing pop off the page. Let's help them.

Introducing the Craft Element: Details

Begin your mini-lesson on details like this:

Teacher: Please listen to this sentence carefully: *The happy boy stood there.*
Do you have any questions for me?

Students: Where is the boy standing? Why is he happy? Why is he standing there?

Teacher: Good questions. I now realize that I didn't give you enough details. That's why you had some questions for me. Let me give you more information through details. Please listen carefully. *The captain of the winning Little League team stood behind the players as the newspaper reporter took their picture.* Let me say that again.

Repeat the sentence for children.

Teacher: Now, I have a couple of questions for you. First, where is the boy standing?

Student: Behind his Little League team.

Teacher: Why is the boy happy?

Student: Because his team just won.

Teacher: Why is he standing behind his team?

Student: Because the newspaper reporter is taking their picture.

Teacher: One last question: Is my first or second sentence more interesting?

Students: The second one. The first one wasn't interesting at all. The second one told us all kinds of things.

Teacher: I'd like to do that one more time. Only this time I'll say the boring sentence and all of you can add details and make it more interesting. Let me think of a sentence that doesn't have details. Just a minute.

Let the class see you thinking and taking your time to come up with a good sentence.

Teacher: OK, I think I have one: *The girl's heart beat really hard.* What are some questions you have?

Student: What's making her heart beat hard?

Student: Where is the girl?

Teacher: Those are two good questions. Now I'd like you to think of a sentence with details that will tell us what is making the girl's heart beat hard and where she is. Details add information—interesting information—that the reader enjoys. For the next three minutes, let's all sit quietly and think. I'll be thinking of an interesting sentence, too.

Again, let the class see you think. (I always shut my eyes while I think. Many of the children do, too.)

Teacher: Did anyone think of a sentence with details?

Student: *When the girl saw the bear outside her tent, her heart beat hard.*

Student: *The girl's dog ran into the street and her heart beat hard.*

Student: *The loud noise frightened the girl and her heart pounded.*

Teacher: Those are great sentences. Can you tell us where she is?

Student: *The loud noise at the circus frightened the girl and her heart pounded.*

Teacher: Thank you for revising your sentence for us. Now I can see where she is.

Leave Room for Details

❊

From the first day of school, I encourage all children to skip two or three lines as they write. I don't tell them why. I ask. They know. They tell me that if they leave room, they'll have a place to add information. Some children say that skipping lines makes it easier for them to read their printing. When they skip lines, there is no way to confuse a first draft with a final draft. It looks like a work in progress. For all of these reasons, skipping lines is a good habit to put into practice.

Student: *The girl got lost in the woods at dark and her heart beat hard.*

Teacher: These were excellent sentences with details that answered your questions.

Student: What's yours? Did you think of a sentence?

Teacher: Yes, I did. *The girl's heart banged in her chest when she saw the snake slither toward her in the lake.* We did a great job of adding details. Do you think our sentences were more interesting than *The girl's heart beat really hard*?

Children nod their heads yes.

Teacher: This year as you write, I want you to stop and reread your first drafts. Sometimes when we are in a hurry to write down our ideas, we forget to add details. But don't worry. We can always add details to make our writing interesting. A good way to find sentences that need details is to read your writing to friends. If they have questions for you, you might consider adding more details to answer those questions.

Mini-Lesson: Details

Part 1: Using Details in a Personal Narrative

Place Overhead 11 (page 51) on the overhead projector. Show sample #1, covering the other writing sample beneath it. Read this piece out loud with expression for general comprehension. Read it again so children become familiar with the content. Then ask these questions:

- Did you hear details in this personal narrative?

- Can you tell me some groups of words that gave you interesting information?

As children offer details, invite them to the overhead projector to underline them. They will mention and underline some or all of these details:

last Tuesday	*with a small rubber hammer*
for my checkup	*my legs jump up*
stethoscope in my ears	*almost accidentally kicked her*
thump, thump, thumpity, thump	*on my tiptoes*
quiet as snow	*again with my eyes closed*
"Aaaaah"	*reaching inside the surprise bag*
deep into my throat	*a glow-in-the-dark sticker*

Ask children: *Do you think this writing was interesting? Did it have details?* Children will tell you that they thought it was an interesting piece of writing and that, yes, it did have quite a few details.

Now show sample #2, cover sample #1, and repeat the process described above. Children will mention (and underline) some or all of these details:

for my checkup

my legs flew up

something from the surprise bag

When you ask whether this writing was interesting and full of details, children will tell you that it had a couple of details, but not very many, and that they didn't think it was all that interesting. For a quick comparison, ask children to count the underlined phrases in sample #1 and in sample #2.

After reading and discussing these two pieces of writing, show both samples on the overhead projector and ask: *Which piece of writing is the more interesting? Which one has more details?* Children will tell you that sample #1 has more details. This will be the piece they enjoy. Encourage them to model their own writing after this piece.

Before ending this mini-lesson, ask children to name their favorite details from sample #1. In this set, they will probably choose *thump, thump, thumpity, thump* and *almost accidentally kicked her*. Whatever their favorites, watch for similar phrases to pop up in their pieces soon.

Part 2: Using Details in Descriptive Writing

Place Overhead 12 (page 52) on the overhead projector. Cover the bottom sample while you and your students examine sample #1. Read it out loud with expression for general comprehension. Read the sample aloud a second time so children become familiar with the content. Then ask these questions:

- Did you hear details in this descriptive piece?

- Can you tell me some groups of words that gave you interesting information?

As children offer details, invite them to the overhead projector to underline them. They will mention and underline some or all of these details in sample #1:

the doll belonged to my mom when she was a girl

wears a blue suit

got some fuzz and some bare spots

two ears that lean to the side

small tail that she usually sits on

Bunny-doll sits on a shelf in my bedroom

Ask children: *Do you think this writing was interesting? Did it have details?* Most children will say that some of it was interesting and it did have details.

Now show sample #2 on the overhead projector and repeat the process described above. Children will mention (and underline) some or all of these details:

one of my mom's keepsakes that she gave to me

no bigger than the inside of my hand

she sits on a shelf above my bed

faded blue suit with a few patches of fuzz

two ears, lined with pink satin

droop to the side from years of play

small white tail serves as a stool

blue eyes open when she sits up

close when she lies back

painted red lips form a small smile

sits quietly watching my every move

once she was my mom's friend, now she is mine

When you ask them to evaluate the writing, children will tell you that it was interesting and it had many details. For a quick comparison, ask children to count the underlined phrases in sample #1 and in sample #2.

After reading and discussing these two pieces of writing, display both on the overhead projector and ask children: *Which piece of writing is more interesting? Which one has more details?* Children will tell you that sample #2 has more details. This will be the piece they enjoy. Encourage them to model their own writing after this piece.

Before ending this mini-lesson, ask children to name their favorite details from sample #2. These are two that children often tell me they enjoy the most: *no bigger than the inside of my hand* and *once she was my mom's friend, now she is mine.* (This particular mini-lesson carries great impact because I bring my bunny-doll with me to show the children. If you have a keepsake from your childhood, consider writing your own two samples with and without details. Children are even more attentive and responsive when they know that the writing has an honest origin.)

Literature Links

For additional mini-lessons, read passages from these books and ask children to mention details that they hear that are interesting to them:

Do You Have a Hat? by Eileen Spinelli

The Girl on the High-Diving Horse by Linda Oatman High

When Riddles Come Rumbling by Rebecca Kai Dotlich

Reteaching Points

If children hesitate or cannot tell you which sample in a set has more detail, make a list of the interesting phrases that they have chosen for each piece on the overhead projector. Give a group of children the transparency of the writing samples with the underlined details. Ask them to read the details to you one at a time. After you have the lists compiled, compare which set has more interesting details—details that the reader wouldn't be able to know or guess unless the writer wrote them. Children like this exercise, and every time they hear the language of detail it helps build a foundation for their own use of specific detail in their pieces.

Details: An Overview of the Craft Element

1. Specific word choice helps build detail. (*two ears, lined with pink satin, droop to the side*)

2. Describing sounds, sights, smells, tastes, or what a person touches help build detail. (*I said, "Aaaaah," and she used a tongue depressor to look deep into my throat*)

3. Describing how a person or thing moves can create detail. (*Blue eyes open when she sits up and close when she lies back*)

4. Using interesting comparisons for size, shape, or color can add detail. (*no bigger than the inside of my hand*)

TIPS FOR WRITERS

What Can You Do to Add Details to Your Writing?

1. Choose specific words to make your writing interesting and add detail.

2. Ask a friend to read or listen to your writing. Have him or her ask you questions about what is happening in your writing. Answer the questions and decide if you want to add details to your piece that would provide this information.

3. Read each sentence in your writing and ask yourself these questions:
   - What happened?
   - How did it happen?
   - What does this sound, look, taste, smell, or feel like?
   - What other information could I tell my reader?

Doctor Visit   1

Last Tuesday, I visited Doctor Watson for my checkup. She started by placing the stethoscope in my ears. I listened to my heart go *thump, thump, thumpity, thump*. After that, I sat as quiet as snow while she listened to my heart and lungs. Next I said, "Aaaaah," and she used a tongue depressor to look deep into my throat. The doctor also examined my ears and eyes. She tapped my knees with a small rubber hammer. It made my legs jump up. One time, I almost accidentally kicked her. She asked me to walk back and forth on my tiptoes. I did it once with my eyes open and again with my eyes closed. It was easy. Of course, my favorite part of the exam was reaching inside the surprise bag. Last Tuesday, I walked out of Dr. Watson's office with a great checkup report and a glow-in-the-dark sticker.

Doctor Visit   2

I went to see Doctor Watson for my checkup. She let me listen to my heart. Then she listened to my heart and lungs. She checked my throat, my ears, and my eyes. Later, she tapped my knees and my legs flew up. I also walked back and forth on the floor. When it was all over the doctor told me I had a great checkup. She let me take something from the surprise bag.

My Old Doll ⓵

I have a doll. I call her Bunny-doll. She's old. The doll belonged to my mom when she was a girl. She's small, too. The doll wears a blue suit that's got some fuzz and some bare spots. She has two ears that lean to the side. The doll has a small tail that she usually sits on. Her face is pretty. She has painted lips and eyes. Her eyes open and close. Bunny-doll sits on a shelf in my bedroom.

Bunny-doll ⓶

Bunny-doll is one of my mom's keepsakes that she gave to me. No bigger than the inside of my hand, she sits on a shelf above my bed. She has a faded blue suit with a few patches of fuzz. Two ears, lined with pink satin, droop to the side from years of play. Her small white tail serves as a stool. But it's her face that I love most. Blue eyes open when she sits up and close when she lies back. Painted red lips form a small smile. Bunny-doll sits quietly watching my every move. Once she was my mom's friend, now she is mine.

CHAPTER 7

Leads

Do You Want to Read On?

To lead means "to guide or show the way." A lead in a piece of writing does just that. Leads are the first words that an audience reads. They set the tone for the piece and show the reader what the writing is about. Leads written with energy and excitement make readers want to read on. Uninteresting ones make the reader want to stop. Let's help student writers craft leads that are both inviting and interesting.

Introducing the Craft Element: Leads

Begin your mini-lesson like this:

Teacher: How many of you have had family or friends come to your home?

Many children will raise their hands or nod their heads yes.

Teacher: How many of you have had family or friends come to your home for a holiday meal?

Some children will raise their hands or announce which relatives or friends come for certain holidays or celebrations.

Teacher: I have some questions for you about how you prepare for and greet your guests. First of all, how do you prepare your home when you know guests are coming for a meal?

Students: We clean up the house. We wash all the dishes. My mom gets out her nice dishes for Thanksgiving dinner. I tie up the dog. We vacuum and dust the house. Dad mows the grass.

Teacher: It sounds as if you all like to greet your guests with a clean and neat home.

Most children will nod their heads in agreement.

Teacher: I have another question. When your guests arrive, how do you greet them at the door?

Students: We open the door and smile. We're all cleaned up, too, and we act nice. My mom opens the door and asks them in. We say "happy birthday" if someone is having a birthday! Yeah, we say "happy Thanksgiving" or "happy Hannukah." Sometimes I tell them what we're having for dinner. At first we all hug. We tell them that we're glad to see them.

Teacher: So let me see if I understand what all of you are saying. When you greet your family and friends, you're smiling and in a good mood.

Children nod yes.

Teacher: Since you've invited them, they know why they are there.

More nods.

Teacher: Most of the time you've invited your guests for a special occasion and you often announce that occasion as they enter.

Students: Yes, that's right.

Teacher: Sometimes you tell them what you're having for dinner or what's going to happen while they're at your home.

More nods of agreement.

Teacher: Well, guess what? As writers, we greet our readers, too. We do it right at the beginning of our piece of writing. In the first few sentences, which are called a lead, we invite our readers into the writing. We tell them a little bit about our topic so they want to know more. And, just as you clean up and put on some of your better clothes when you greet guests, a writer uses some of his best words, to greet his reader. He makes his lead as interesting as possible so his audience will want to read more. The lead is a time for the writer to say, "Welcome to my writing. I think you're going to like it."

Mini-Lesson: Leads

Part 1: Introducing a Personal Narrative

Place Overhead 13 (page 60) on the overhead projector. Cover the second and third writing samples in this set. Read sample #1 out loud with expression for general comprehension. Read it again so children become familiar with the content. Then ask these questions:

- Does this lead give you some basic information about the writing in an interesting way?
- Does the lead make you want to read on?

Children will tell you that this lead does offer some basic information. They learn about the chirping sound and where it's coming from. They learn that the narrator went in the barn and saw a bird. Is it interesting? Some children will say yes, others will not know. That's just fine. Quite often it's the comparison with other leads that helps them identify the strongest. Most children will say that they do want to read on to find out why the bird needs help.

Display sample #2 on the overhead projector. Repeat the process described above. Children will tell you that this lead offers more information than the last one. They will appreciate the sound effect *Peep! Peep!* Most children will tell you that this lead is more interesting than the last lead. And now, all children will tell you that they would like to hear more of this piece.

Now show sample #3 on the overhead projector. Repeat the process described above. Children will tell you that this lead offers the least amount of information and it isn't all that interesting. Some will say that they would still like to read on, but most will say they would prefer not to read on after this lead.

For a quick comparison, display all three leads on the overhead projector at the same time. Reread them again if the children need that extra support. Then ask: *Which of these three leads makes you want to read on the most?* Children will say that sample #2 is the lead that makes them want to read on the most. This will be the lead they enjoy. Encourage them to model their own leads after this one.

Part 2: Introducing a Nonfiction Piece

Place Overhead 14 (page 61) on the overhead projector. Cover the second and third writing samples and read sample #1 out loud with expression for general comprehension. Read it again so children become familiar with the content. Then ask these questions:

- Does this lead give you some basic information about the writing in an interesting way?
- Does the lead make you want to read on?

Children will tell you that there is some basic information about bicycles in this lead. Most children will tell you that the information isn't too interesting, though, and they really don't want to read more after this lead.

Place sample #2 on the overhead projector. Repeat the process described above. Children will tell you that this lead gives a little information about bicycles, but not much. Again, they will say that it is not very interesting and they wouldn't necessarily want to read more.

Place sample #3 on the overhead projector. Repeat the process described above. This time, children will say that this lead has quite a bit of information. Ask them, *What do you learn about the first bicycles?* They will mention that

> *the first bicycles were made of iron and wood*
>
> *they were built in the 1800s*
>
> *they were not sleek or comfortable*
>
> *just about everyone back then wanted one*

Children will say that this information is interesting. They like knowing that many people wanted a bicycle back then. They will also say that they now would want to read more about these first bicycles. If people wanted them, they'd like to know why. Show all three of the leads on the overhead projector at once. Ask children to point out which lead is the most interesting and most makes them want to read on. All children will say that sample #3 is the best lead. It definitely makes them want to read on. Encourage children to model their own leads after this interesting example.

Part 3: Introducing a Story

Place Overhead 15 (page 62) on the overhead projector. Cover the second and third sample leads and read sample #1 out loud with expression for general comprehension. Read it again so children become familiar with the content. Then ask these questions:

- Does this lead give you some basic information about the writing in an interesting way?
- Does the lead make you want to read on?

Children will say that this lead gives lots of information. Ask them: *What do you know about this story already?* The children will tell you that they know the story is about a wolf and that he thinks he is going to eat three plump rabbits for dinner. Children will also tell you that the lead is interesting. They hear how he licked his chops and what he thought. Most children will say that they want to read more.

Show sample #2 on the overhead projector, covering the others. Repeat the process described above. Children will say that this lead has basic information, but it is not written in an interesting way. Most children will tell you that this lead does not make them want to read more; in fact, it sounds as if the writing is complete. There's no reason to read on.

Show sample #3 on the overhead projector, covering the others. Repeat the process described above. Children will again say that this lead has basic information but isn't all that interesting. Most children would not read on after this lead.

Display all three samples on the overhead projector and ask: *Which lead has interesting information and makes you want to read on?* Most children will immediately say that sample #1 is the best lead of this group. It is the one that makes them want to read on. Again, encourage children to model their leads after this engaging story lead.

Part 4: Introducing Procedural Writing

Place Overhead 16 (page 63) on the overhead projector. Cover the second writing sample in this set. Read sample #1 out loud with expression for general comprehension. Read it again so children become familiar with the content. Then ask these questions:

- Does this lead give you some basic information about the writing in an interesting way?
- Does the lead make you want to read on?

Children will tell you that this lead has basic information. They will also say that it isn't written in an interesting way. Half of the children will want to read on because of the content; the other half will say that they wouldn't read on.

Cover sample #1 and uncover sample #2. Repeat the process described above. Children will mention that this lead also offers basic information but is more interesting. The title and directions use stronger vocabulary that is more specific. Most children will say that they would want to read on after sample #2.

Show both leads on the overhead projector and ask children which one has more interesting information and makes them want to read on. Almost every student will say that sample #2 is the better lead. Encourage children to model their leads in procedural writing after this one.

Reteaching Points

If children cannot tell you which lead in a set is the best, put that transparency back on the overhead projector and ask the children to underline all the interesting information in each lead. This will be a quick visual for them to see that leads with interesting details are the ones that make us want to read more. See page 59 for examples of personal narrative leads with interesting information highlighted.

Leads: An Overview of the Craft Element

1. Specific word choice makes a lead more interesting. (*iron and wood bicycles of the 1800s*)

2. All leads need basic information, including the who and what. (*Wolf awoke from his nap hungrier than usual; Looking around, he spotted three plump rabbits hopping toward the garden*)

3. Adding a few details to a lead can make it more interesting. (*Peep! Peep!, young swallow perched on the side of its nest*)

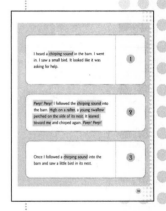

The highlighted words and phrases on page 59 show which of the three samples on the Leads overhead on page 60 has the most detail.

4. The interesting details invite or guide readers into the writing. (*they were one of the most desired inventions of the time*)

5. A good lead will make the reader want to read more.

How Can You Write a Strong Lead?

1. Study leads in published writing. Note the interesting details and the information that makes you want to read on.
2. Use specific word choice in your lead.
3. Check that your lead has the basic information of who and what.
4. Make sure that your lead has at least two interesting details.
5. Read your lead to a writer friend and ask, "Do you want to hear more?"

I heard a chirping sound in the barn. I went in. I saw a small bird. It looked like it was asking for help.

1

Peep! Peep! I followed the chirping sound into the barn. High on a rafter, a young swallow perched on the side of its nest. It leaned toward me and chirped again. *Peep! Peep!*

2

Once I followed a chirping sound into the barn and saw a little bird in its nest.

3

1

I heard a chirping sound in the barn. I went in. I saw a small bird. It looked like it was asking for help.

2

Peep! Peep! I followed the chirping sound into the barn. High on a rafter, a young swallow perched on the side of its nest. It leaned toward me and chirped again. *Peep! Peep!*

3

Once I followed a chirping sound into the barn and saw a little bird in its nest.

1

The first bicycles were different. They were large and uncomfortable.

2

The first bicycles of the 1800s looked nothing like today's bikes, nor were they as comfortable.

3

The first iron and wood bicycles of the 1800s were anything but sleek and comfortable. Nevertheless, they were one of the most desired inventions of the time.

1

Wolf awoke from his nap hungrier than usual. Looking around, he spotted three plump rabbits hopping toward the garden. Wolf licked his chops. Dinner looks mighty good tonight, he thought.

2

Wolf was hungry. He saw three large rabbits. He decided to eat them for dinner.

3

Wolf woke from his nap. He wondered what he'd have for dinner. Then he saw three plump rabbits. He ran toward them.

How to Make a Canoe Go 1

stuff you need: canoe

paddle

life vest

directions: Put your paddle in.

Put on your vest.

Push your canoe.

How to Paddle a Canoe 2

equipment: life vest

canoe

paddle

directions: Put on your life vest.

Place the paddle in the canoe.

Slowly push the canoe into the water.

CHAPTER 8

Revision

THE QUESTION TO EXPLORE

How Can I Improve My Writing?

All children know the difference between quality writing and sloppy, or poor, writing. They are excited to learn revision strategies that they can use to improve the meaning of their work. They enjoy identifying weak and passive verbs and replacing them with strong, active verbs that show how something happened. They ask themselves questions to add details for interest and information. They revisit their work to write inviting leads and satisfying endings. But revision, like any other aspect of the writing craft, needs to be taught and modeled. When that happens, children understand that improving their writing is an important and welcome part of the writing process.

Introducing the Craft Element: Revision

Begin your mini-lesson on revision like this:

Teacher: I just remembered something that I saw this morning on my way into school. Please listen and watch as I get my idea written so I don't forget it.

Think out loud so the children can hear your thinking process.

Teacher: OK, I want to put down my thoughts on the flag that was whipping around in the wind. I remember that it seemed to be a doing a kind of dance and the morning sun was like a spotlight shining on it.

Read your sentence out loud as you write it.

Teacher: **The American flag jumped in the morning light.**

> Hmmm, that's not exactly what I wanted to say, but I did get my general idea down on paper. Maybe you can help me. I remember that I thought the flag was dancing. What are some nouns—naming words—that name or describe different kinds of dances?

Students: *Break dancing. Tap dance. Shuffle. Flap. Do-si-do. Ballet. Plié. Jump. Twist. Turn. Twirl.*

Teacher: I can't believe you thought of that many different dances or dance moves! Now I need to think. The term *tap dance* actually describes the snapping of the flag this morning. I think that word works much better than *jumped*.

> Since I'm talking about the American flag, I want to think about why it could be tap dancing. Oh, it could be saluting the morning. I like that idea. It sounds snappy, like the flag. OK, *The American flag tap-danced a morning salute to the sun.* I like that. Let me write it down.

Write the second sentence beneath your first sentence.

Teacher: **The American flag tap-danced a morning salute to the sun.**
Tell me words that you think are stronger in my revision than in my first sentence.

Student: I like *tap-danced* better than *jumped*.

Student: I like how you added *salute*.

Student: Yeah, I've seen soldiers salute the flag at parades, but you have the flag saluting the sun.

Student: I can see the flag doing this.

Teacher: Do you think my revisions improved my writing?

Children nod their heads in agreement.

Teacher: Thank you. I do, too. That's why we revisit our writing. At first we simply get our ideas down on paper. Then we go back and play with the words to improve our meaning—to help it say exactly what was in our mind. This year we will take time to revisit our writing and rethink what it says. All writers revise. Everyone wants their writing to be the best it can be.

Mini-Lesson: Revision

Part 1: Revising for Meaning

Place Overhead 17 (page 75) on the overhead projector. Covering samples B through D, read sentence A out loud with expression for general comprehension. Read it again so the children become familiar with its content. Then ask:

- Do you understand all of this sentence?

Children will tell you that they know a dog bit and chewed something. What they don't know or understand is what *it* was. Ask:

- What could it have been?

Children will say it could have been a ball, a shoe, a piece of clothing, a book, a CD, etc. Continue modeling like this:

Teacher: I'm going to revise this sentence. I'm going to rewrite it and improve it by telling my audience what the dog bit and chewed.

Let the children hear you think out loud.

Teacher: We've had plenty of puppies and dogs over the years. I know the kinds of things they like to chew. I'm going to have this dog biting a rug . . . no . . . a welcome mat, and then I'm going to describe how the mat looked.

Read your sentence out loud as you write it.

Teacher: **The puppy bit and chewed the welcome mat until it became a puddle of colored dust.**
Now, I'd like all of you to write your revision of this sentence. You may add another detail, too, if you wish. You may write where this happened, or how the dog bit and chewed. You may even add some sound words to show the noise that the dog made while biting and chewing.

Provide three or four minutes for the revision, then another three or four minutes for children to share with a writing buddy. Encourage the class to celebrate one improvement they hear in their partner's revision.

Repeat this process for samples B through D on other days for an interactive mini-lesson. Nudge children toward revision by always asking whether they understand all of the writing. When they mention a confusing place, brainstorm options to improve the meaning. Questions you may ask include:

- What is *it*? (sample B)
- What is the sound? Can you describe how loud it was and why it was bad? (sample C)
- Where is *there*? Be specific and tell why the plant likes that place so much. (sample D)

Sample Writing: Revision for Meaning

Place Overhead 17 on the overhead projector again. Cover examples A through D so that only Passage 1 is showing. Read it out loud with expression for general comprehension. Read it again so the children become familiar with its content. Now, go back and reread the first sentence. Ask children:

- Do you understand everything in the writing?

Tip

A lways remember to begin each of these interactive mini-lessons with your own modeling. Introducing revision in this non-threatening manner gives children confidence and strategies to revise not only the samples in this book but their own writing in the future.

Circle any words or phrases—like the word *he*—that children find confusing. Repeat this process for each sentence in the passage. On a separate transparency have children brainstorm specific words for *he* and *him* that would add more meaning to the piece of writing. Their list might include suggestions similar to these:

> *Tabby the cat*
>
> *our tiger cat*
>
> *our pet, Dickens*
>
> *Susie, our dog*
>
> *the watchdog*

Place the writing sample with the circled words back on the overhead projector. Ask children to revise the sample using specific nouns for the words that they found confusing. If a child wants to add a few more details, encourage him or her to do so. In that way, the child takes ownership over the revision process.

Provide 8 to 12 minutes for your class to rewrite the sample. (Make sure that you are revising the passage at this time, as well.) Then provide another four to five minutes for children to share their revisions with a writing partner. (Again, select a partner and share your revision, too.) Encourage children to celebrate any revisions that have improved the meaning of the sample.

Your revised sample might look something like this:

> *Our house cat, Griffin, followed the mouse through the house, ready to pounce. The mouse scurried behind the refrigerator. Griffin waited close by. Hour after hour passed and eventually our big gray cat fell fast asleep. In the middle of the night, the mouse hurried past the dozing cat for a midnight snack of crumbs. YUM!*

Part 2: Revising for Word Choice

Place Overhead 18 (page 76) on the overhead projector so that only sample A shows. Read the sentence out loud with expression for general comprehension. Read it again so children become familiar with the content. Ask:

- Do these words paint a picture?

Children will tell you that most of the words do not paint a vivid picture. Ask them to mention and circle the weak and general words. Train children to always look at the verb(s) first. Since strong, active verbs help create pictures in the mind of the reader, we want children to always stop and consider the verb choice. Ask, *Does the word* put *paint a specific picture in your mind?* When they tell you that it does not paint a specific picture, ask for words that might show exactly what the student did with the paper. Children might brainstorm: *pushed, slid, slipped, guided, shoved, jammed.*

Continue examining the other vocabulary in sample A. Ask children to look at the nouns next—the words that name people, places, or things. Are these words specific? Do they paint pictures? The children will typically circle *paper* and *door*

Tools for the Teacher

Introducing children to meaningful revision takes patience, consistency, and celebration. Here are two professional books that will provide you with solid tools to show children the satisfaction to be gained through revision:

Making Revision Matter by Janet Angelillo

The Revision Toolbox by Georgia Heard

as weak vocabulary. Sometimes, they will circle *student* as well, because they want the name of a particular child. Brainstorm specific replacements for these vague words. Children might offer

> *student—Amy, Jeff, Grant, the first-grade student*
>
> *paper—letter, report card, note, envelope, e-mail, question, apology*
>
> *door—principal's office door, bathroom door, classroom door, detention room door, closed door, locked door, private door*

Continue modeling like this:

Teacher: I'm going to revise this sentence for stronger word choice. I'm going to rewrite it and try to paint a specific picture with my words.

Let children hear you think out loud.

Teacher: I think I'd like the paper to be an invitation. Since the sentence says *student*, I want him to be inviting another class to his classroom for some special event—like a play, or Readers Theater. Oh, I know— how about for a science event? So, I want my student to be a boy named . . . Rory, and I think the invitation is folded, so it has some weight to it. I think I picture him on his hands and knees flicking his finger against it and the invitation scoots across the floor.

Since it is another classroom, I think it will be the closed door of Room 242. I think I'm ready to write.

Read your sentence out loud as you write it.

Teacher: **Rory knelt down and flicked the invitation to his Paper Airplane Fly-Off under the closed door of Room 242.** Now I'd like all of you to write your revision of this sentence. You can make the student be anyone you like. Think before you write. What is the paper? How is the student putting it under the door? What kind of door is it?

Provide three or four minutes for the revision, then another three or four minutes for children to share with a writing partner. (Select a partner, too, and share your revision.) Encourage the class to celebrate one improvement they hear in their partner's revision.

Repeat this process for samples B through D on other days for an interactive mini-lesson. Nudge children toward revision by always asking: *Do these words paint a picture?* When children mention weak vocabulary, brainstorm options to improve the word choice. Questions you might ask include

- What could be more specific than *boat, moved,* or *water?* (sample B)
- What could be more specific than *sun, made,* or *hot?* (sample C)
- What could be more specific than *animal, went,* and *tree?* (sample D)

Sample Writing: Revising for Word Choice

Place Overhead 18 on the overhead projector again so that only Passage 2 is showing. Read the passage out loud with expression for general comprehension. Read it again so the children become familiar with its content. Ask:

- Do all of these words paint a picture?

Circle any words or phrases that children think are weak and could be replaced with more specific alternatives. Their list might include

> *was colorful*
>
> *hung*
>
> *fell*
>
> *from the tree*
>
> *blew*
>
> *all over the yard*
>
> *ended up*
>
> *pile*
>
> *other leaves*

Place the writing sample with the circled words back on the overhead projector. Ask children to revise the sample using more specific verbs and nouns. Remind the class to also add phrases that will paint pictures for the reader. Provide 8 to 12 minutes, or longer if needed, for children to rewrite the sample. (Make sure that they can see you revising the sample as well.)

Then provide another four or five minutes for them to share their revisions with a writing partner. (Select a partner, too, and share your revision.) Encourage children to celebrate any word-choice revisions that have helped to paint stronger pictures.

Your revised sample might look like this:

Autumn's red and orange speckled the crinkled leaf as it danced in the wind at the end of a branch. One cool morning, it broke free and slowly twirled and swirled to the ground. The stiff leaf skipped across the yard until it was reunited with friends from above. They sat huddled together, whispering fall's secrets.

Part 3: Revising for Details

Place Overhead 19 (page 77) on the overhead projector so that only sample A is showing. Read the sentence out loud with expression for general comprehension. Read it again so children become familiar with its content. Now ask:

- Does this writing have interesting details?

Children will tell you that the sentence does not have interesting details. Ask them what they would like to know. Children will say something like this: *How did the sister go into the lake? What's her name? Did she make any noise?*

Continue modeling like this:

Teacher: Those are all good questions. I agree with you. I think this sentence can be revised and be much more interesting. I'm going to revise it right now. But first I need to think.

Let the children hear you think out loud.

Teacher: I see a girl excited to be at the lake. So she rushes in, maybe even does some cartwheels as she crosses the sand. I think she would grab her knees and jump into the deeper water, making a big splash that showers water over others. OK, I'm ready to work on my revision.

Read your sentence out loud as you write it.

Teacher: **My show-off sister Clara cartwheeled across the beach, stopped at the water's edge, and cannonballed into the lake, splashing everyone who dared to be near her.**

Now, I'd like all of you to write your revision of this sentence. Add details that will create interest for the reader.

Provide three or four minutes for the revision, then another three or four minutes for children to share with a writing partner. Encourage the class to celebrate one improvement they hear in their partner's revision.

Repeat this process for samples B through D on other days for an interactive mini-lesson. Nudge children toward revision by always asking them what questions they have about each sentence. Questions you may ask include:

- What kind of flowers are they? How did they look pretty? Were they in a garden, a vase? (sample B)

- What kind of book is it? How do we know it's been read a lot? Are the pages torn? Is the cover loose? (sample C)

- What kind of dinner was it? What made it so good? Was it tasty? (sample D)

Sample Writing: Revising for Details

Place Overhead 19 on the overhead projector again so that only Passage 3 is showing. Read the passage out loud with expression for general comprehension. Read it again so children become familiar with its content. Now go back and reread the first sentence.

Ask children: *Do you have any questions for the writer?* They will respond with a question such as *What kind of cookies?* You might put a question mark above the word *cookies* and write the word *kind*.

Continue questioning words and phrases that lack specificity in the rest of the piece. Some questions from children may include *How did the writer's mom help? What stuff did the writer put in the bowl? How did they mix it up? How did they put them in the oven? How many cookies did they each eat? Where were they when eating the cookies? What made these cookies the best ever?*

Keep the transparency on the overhead projector with the question marks and simple notes that you have added per their questions. Ask children to revise the sample passage by adding some interesting details about making cookies. While they are writing, sit and write your own revision of this piece. Provide 8 to 12 minutes for children to rewrite the sample. Then provide another four or five minutes for them to share their revisions with a writing partner. Select a writing partner, too, and share your revision. Encourage children to celebrate any revisions that added interesting details.

Your revised piece might look like this:

Last week, I learned how to make Snickerdoodles. My mom read me the recipe and asked me if I wanted to make them with her. "Sure," I said. So we found all of the ingredients and measured them carefully. Next, we put the butter, sugar, eggs, milk, and vanilla into a bowl and mixed them with the electric beaters. Whirr! Whirr! We added the dry ingredients one by one and mixed it all together until it was smooth. We dropped the dough by teaspoons onto the cookie sheet and baked them in the oven. Later, the sugar melted on our tongues as we ate cookies under the stars.

Part 4: Revising for Organization

Place Overhead 20 (page 78) on the overhead projector and begin your mini-lesson like this:

Teacher: Remember how informational writing has a lead or beginning, at least three interesting pieces of information in the middle, and an ending? Today we're going to read about horseshoe crabs. (*pointing to the title on the transparency*) See, "Horseshoe Crabs" is the title. Now we know the topic of the writing. Unfortunately, this writing has been jumbled up. We're going to find the beginning, the middles, and the end and write it in the correct organizational order. Let me read all of the sentences so you know what the writing is about.

Read the sentences on the transparency out loud with expression for general comprehension.

Teacher: Now, I'd like to read them again. Start thinking about what sounds like the beginning, or the lead, of this piece.

Read the sentences out loud again so the children become familiar with the content.

Teacher: We know this is about horseshoe crabs, but what is the author mostly explaining in this piece?

Student: Their shells.

Student: Yeah, they can grow out of them.

Student: And they protect them.

Student: The shells are big and brown.

Teacher: What's another name for their shells?

Student: *Exoskeleton.*

Teacher: You all are reading and listening well today. These sentences have been grouped together in pairs. So we need to find the two sentences that are the beginning of this piece. Which sentences introduce horseshoe crabs to us? Which sentences first mention the shells?

Student: Not the first pair—the second pair of sentences.

Teacher: (reading) *Horseshoe crabs are animals that live in the ocean and nest on land. They are unusual animals because they have big, brown shells that look like helmets.* Does that sound like an introduction to the crabs and their shells?

Children nod their heads in agreement.

Teacher: Could someone please come up here and write a capital *B* in front of those two sentences?

A volunteer marks the section.

Teacher: Thank you. Sometimes it's easier to look next for the ending. An author usually wraps up the writing at the end or tells us another piece of general information about the topic. Let me read the sentences again, minus the beginning, and see if you can find two sentences that sound like the ending, as if the writer is bringing everything together.

Read the first, third, and last groups of sentences out loud again.

Teacher: Does anyone see anything that looks and sounds like an ending?

Student: Most of the sentences talk about the shell. But the third group tells the reader not to be afraid. It tells us again how horseshoe crabs live in the ocean. Is that the ending?

Teacher: Yes, I think it is. Would you please come up to the overhead projector and write a capital *E* in front of those two sentences?

A volunteer marks the section.

Teacher: Thank you. Now we only have two groups of sentences left. We need to decide which group will follow the lead. Let me read our beginning again.

Read the two sentences identified as the beginning to the class.

Teacher: Now let me read the first group of sentences and you decide if it flows from our beginning.

Read the first two sentences of the writing sample out loud.

Teacher: Now, let me read the beginning again and I'll read the last two sentences on the page.

Reread the beginning out loud, then the last two sentences on the page.

Teacher: What do you think? Do you think the first two sentences work better right after the beginning, or the last two?

Student: It seems like either one could go next.

Student: Yes, but the first two sentences tell us that their shells are exoskeletons. I think we need that one first.

Teacher: What do all of you think?

Students: It needs to be the first two sentences, then the last two. Uh-huh, that's right. Yes.

Teacher: I agree with your decision. I need someone to come up here and mark those middle sections M 1 and M 2 to show the order we agreed on. Now we have all of our parts marked.

Point to each section as you name it.

Teacher: We have a beginning, two middle sections that give us four pieces of interesting information, and our ending.

Horseshoe Crabs

M 1   These shells are really exoskeletons.

Their exoskeletons protect their bodies from harm.

....

B   Horseshoe crabs are animals that live in the ocean and nest on land.

They are unusual animals because they have big, brown shells that look like helmets.

....

E   If you ever see a horseshoe crab on the beach, don't be afraid.

They are gentle creatures that live quiet lives in the sea.

....

M 2   As horseshoe crabs age, they outgrow their shells.

So, they crawl out of their exoskeletons and grow new ones that fit their larger bodies.

Teacher: I would like all of us to revise, or rewrite, this informational piece in the correct organizational order. I'll sit here and write mine while all of you write yours. One thing before we begin: When we write a piece, does it look like a list of sentences?

Children shake their heads no.

Teacher: No. So, I would like you to write this as a paragraph, one sentence flowing into the next. Make sure you start with the beginning that you identified.

Provide about 15 minutes for children to reorganize this piece of writing. Also provide five to seven minutes for them to read their revised paragraphs to one another. Reading to an audience is always the best celebration for writing effort.

Your completed piece would look like this:

Horseshoe Crabs

Horseshoe crabs are animals that live in the ocean and nest on land. They are unusual animals because they have big, brown shells that look like helmets. These shells are really exoskeletons. Their exoskeletons protect their bodies from harm. As horseshoe crabs age, they outgrow their shells. So, they crawl out of their exoskeletons and grow new ones that fit their larger bodies. If you ever see a horseshoe crab on the beach, don't be afraid. They are gentle creatures that live quiet lives in the sea.

Revision: An Overview of the Craft Element

1. Revision is a way to clarify the meaning of the writing.

2. Writers replace general words with specific ones to paint pictures in the reader's mind.

3. Writers revise by adding details to inform, entertain, or explain.

4. Writers reorganize so that meaning is clear.

5. Revision helps a writer notice strengths and weaknesses in the piece.

TIPS FOR WRITERS

How Can You Revise to Make Your Writing Stronger?

1. Read your writing out loud to notice any weaknesses.
2. Look for general words and replace them with specific ones.
3. Check that you have details in your writing.
4. Make sure your details paint pictures in the minds of your readers.
5. Identify the beginning, middle (at least three details or pieces of information), and end of your piece.
6. Ask a friend to help you check your piece for vocabulary, details, or organization. (Just one, please, not all.)
7. After you revise, read a portion of your writing to a friend. First, read the writing before revision. Then, read your writing with the revision. Ask your friend what he or she likes better in the revision. Celebrate!

A: The dog bit and chewed it.

B: It was the best one on the table.

C: The sound frightened me. It was loud and bad.

D: Plants always grow better there. They like
     that spot.

Passage 1

He followed the mouse through the house, ready to
pounce. The mouse scurried behind the refrigerator.
He waited close by, hour after hour, until he fell
asleep. In the middle of the night, the mouse hurried
past him for a midnight snack of crumbs. Yum!

A: The student put the paper under the door.

B: The boat moved through the water.

C: The sun made the sidewalk hot.

D: The animal went up the tree.

Passage 2

The leaf was colorful. It hung on a branch. One day it fell from the tree. It blew all over the yard. It ended up in a pile with other leaves.

A: My sister went into the lake.

B: The flowers looked pretty.

C: This book has been read a lot.

D: Mom's dinner was good.

Passage 3

I learned how to make cookies. My mom helped me. We put stuff in a bowl. We mixed it up. We put them in the oven. Later, we ate them. They were the best cookies ever.

Reorganize this piece of writing so it makes sense and flows from one piece of information to the next.

- Find a lead and write it first.

- Write the middle pieces of information.

- Finally, write the ending.

Passage 4

Horseshoe Crabs

These shells are really exoskeletons. Their exoskeletons protect their bodies from harm.

Horseshoe crabs are animals that live in the ocean and nest on land. They are unusual animals because they have big, brown shells that look like helmets.

If you ever see a horseshoe crab on the beach, don't be afraid. They are gentle creatures that live quiet lives in the sea.

As horseshoe crabs age, they outgrow their shells. So, they crawl out of their exoskeletons and grow new ones that fit their larger bodies.

Bibliography

Angelillo, J. (2005). *Making revision matter*. New York: Scholastic.

Cronin, D. (2003). *Diary of a worm*. New York: HarperCollins.

Dotlich, R. K. (2001). *When riddles come rumbling*. Honesdale, PA: Boyds Mills Press.

Fox, M. (1989). *Night noises*. San Diego: Harcourt Brace Jovanovich.

Graham, J. B. (1999). *Flicker flash*. New York: Houghton Mifflin.

Gray, L. M. (1993). *Miss Tizzy*. New York: Simon & Schuster.

Heard, G. (2002). *The revision toolbox: Teaching techniques that work*. Portsmouth, NH: Heinemann.

High, L. O. (2003). *The girl on the high-diving horse*. New York: Philomel.

Lyon, G. E. (2004). *Weaving the rainbow*. New York: Atheneum.

McDonald, M. (2003). *The Judy Moody mood journal*. New York: Candlewick Press.

Park, B. (2003). *Top-secret personal beeswax: A journal by Junie B. (and me!)*. New York: Random House.

Ryan, P. M. (2002). *When Marian sang*. New York: Scholastic.

Schanzer, R. (2001). *Davy Crockett saves the world*. New York: HarperCollins.

Spinelli, E. (2004). *Do you have a hat?* New York: Simon & Schuster.

White, E. B. (1952). *Charlotte's web*. New York: Harper & Row.

Index

details, 45
  descriptive writing and, 48–49, 52
  introducing, 45–47
  mini-lesson, 47–50
  overheads, 51–52
  overview of, 50
  personal narratives and, 47–48, 51
  revision and, 69–71, 77

fiction writing, meaning and, 14–15

focus, 18
  introducing, 18–19
  mini-lesson, 20–22
  narrative writing and, 20–21, 23–24
  nonfiction and, 21
  overheads, 23–24
  overview of, 22

journal writing, 6
  introducing, 6–8
  mini-lesson, 8–10
  overhead, 11
  overview of, 10

leads, 53
  introducing, 53–54
  mini-lesson, 54–58
  nonfiction and, 55–56, 61
  overview of, 57–58
  personal narratives and, 54–55, 59–60
  procedural writing and, 57, 63
  story, 56–57, 62

meaning, 12
  fiction and, 14–15
  introducing, 12–13
  mini-lesson, 14–15
  nonfiction and, 14
  overheads, 16–17
  overview of, 15
  revision and, 65–67, 75

mini-lessons
  details, 47–50
  journal writing, 8–10
  leads, 54–58
  meaning, 14–15
  organization, 27–32
  vocabulary, 38–42

narrative writing, focus and, 20–21, 23–24

nonfiction writing
  focus and, 21
  leads and, 55–56, 61
  meaning and, 14, 16
  organization and, 30–31, 36

organization, 25
  introducing, 25–27
  mini-lesson, 27–32
  nonfiction, 30–31, 36
  overview of, 32
  personal narrative, 27–29, 33–34
  revision and, 71–74, 78
  story, 29–30, 35

overheads (reproducibles)
  details, 51–52
  focus, 23–24
  journal writing, 11
  leads, 60–63
  meaning, nonfiction writing, 16
  organization, 34–36
  revision, 75–78
  vocabulary, 43–44

personal narratives
  details and, 47–48, 51
  leads and, 54–55, 59–60
  organization and, 27–29, 33–34

procedural writing, leads and, 57, 63

revision, 64
  introducing, 64–65
  overheads, 75–78
  overview of, 74

revision, mini-lessons, 65–74
  details, 69–71
  meaning, 65–67
  organization, 71–74
  word choice, 67–69

stories
  leads and, 56–57, 62
  organization and, 29–30, 35

vocabulary, 37
  introducing, 37–38
  mini-lesson, 38–42
  overheads, 43–44
  overview of, 42
  revision and, 67–69, 76

word choice. *See* vocabulary